# BOOK THE JOB

# JOB

## 143 THINGS ACTORS NEED TO KNOW
## TO MAKE IT HAPPEN

# OTHER TITLES BY DOUG WARHIT

## THE ACTOR'S AUDITION CHECKLIST

## WARHIT'S GUIDEBOOK FOR THE ACTOR

## 49 SCENES WITH BITE:
## (PIECES ACTORS CAN SINK THEIR TEETH INTO)

The above titles may be purchased in bulk
at special discount rates by contacting:

**Dau Publishing**
**10650 Holman Ave. Suite 205**
**Los Angeles Ca 90024**
**PHONE: (310) 560-8474**
**FAX: (310) 446-4815**
**Email: Daupub@aol.com**

# BOOK THE JOB

## 143 THINGS ACTORS NEED TO KNOW TO MAKE IT HAPPEN

### DOUG WARHIT
### ACTING COACH

Publishing

**Dau Publishing**
Los Angeles, California

Dau Publishing
10650 Holman Ave. Suite 205
Los Angeles Ca. 90024

Editor: Gladys Itkin
Cover Design & Layout: Declan Geraghty


Publisher's Cataloging-in-Publication Data

Warhit, Doug
        Book the job: 143 things actors need
        to know to make it happen/Doug Warhit
        p. cm.
        ISBN 0-9726262-7-1
        1. Acting-Auditions. 1. Title.
    PN2071.A92 2002
    792'.028-dc21                            02-115111
                                                CIP



Printed in the United States of America

*Dedicated to*

**Gladys Itkin, George Warhit, Billy Keane,
& Brigitta Dau**

*Special thanks to*

**Declan Geraghty, Matt McCoy, Jerry Giordano,
Alexandra Paul, Alex Boling, Dawn Herriott,
Tracy Scoggins, Tina Louise Eckert, Jim O'Brien,
Tina Illman, Casey McFeron, Dan Fauci, Mike Mand,
Alex Wright, Beverly Wiles, Rebecca Mall,
Gillian Combe, Peter Warhit, Ted Baker, Mike Gold,
& Gina Ravera.**

*And to all of the wonderful actors I've been
privileged  to work with*

# CONTENTS

## SECTION ONE: <u>AUDITIONS</u>

### BEFORE THE AUDITION

### During The Audition

## After The Audition

## Agent Auditions

## Commercials

## Expecting The Unexpected

# SECTION TWO: <u>THE BUSINESS</u>

## Diving In

## The Nitty Gritty

## Age Old Questions

## You Never Know

# SECTION THREE: ACTING TECHNIQUE

## Pushing The Envelope

## Hitting The High Notes

## The Pleasure In The Pain

## Did You Say Something?

## The Checklist

# SECTION FOUR: WORKING ON THE SET

## On Your Mark

## Working With The Director

## The Crew

## Extra Work

## Sitcom Sins And Secrets

## Soap Opera Myths

# SECTION FIVE:
# BREAKING FREE OF BARRIERS

## Changing Your Perspective

## Who's Running The Show?

## Stardom

# SECTION ONE: AUDITIONS

*"I always wanted them to like me. Then I finally decided that I had to trust myself, not worry about what they might want. I was going to do it the way I thought it should be done. The challenge was in the work, not pleasing them."*

**-Calista Flockhart**

*"I believed so thoroughly I was going to be a star that whenever I got turned down for something I thought, my God, when are these people going to wake up?"*

**-Richard Dreyfuss**

# BEFORE THE AUDITION

## NO SINGLE AUDITION WILL MAKE OR BREAK YOUR CAREER

*"If I get this part my career will be made." "If I blow it, I'll never get another chance like this again."*

Thinking this way is like going to Las Vegas, betting every penny you have on a single toss of the dice, and then wondering why you're falling apart. Not a good method to prepare unless you thrive on incredible amounts of pressure. Trust that if you do good work, you will book jobs, but don't make any single audition "the be all, end all" of your career. Number one: it won't help you do your best. Number two: it's a lie.

*Some actors will tell you that they're most successful when they don't really care whether they book the job or not. What they're really saying is that they care enough to do good work, but they aren't desperate for the job.*

*Never make any single audition "the be all, end all" of your career. Number one: it won't help you do your best work. Number two: it's a lie.*

# THE NIGHT BEFORE THE AUDITION

Studies have shown that most people only tap into ten percent of their brainpower; the conscious mind. They don't realize that ninety percent of the good stuff is hidden beneath the surface. If you expect to do your best work, you must learn to go deeper.

The night before the audition is particularly important. Ten minutes before you go to sleep, sit in a comfortable chair, close your eyes, and visualize the audition exactly the way you want it to go. Visualize the casting director responding strongly to your work. See her nodding yes, with a big smile on her face. Hear her saying, *"That's it. My gosh, you're a terrific actor."* Next hear your agent saying, *"You got the job!"* Then visualize yourself on the set actually playing the part. See the director and the other actors praising your work. Visualize the producer telling you the studio wants to hire you again. After you finish the visualization, say to yourself, *"Either this or something better."* Then let it go. While you are asleep, your unconscious mind will do everything it can to assist you in creating your desired outcome.

**Note one:** The above exercise should be done in addition to your conscious preparation.

**Note two:** Even if you aren't told about the audition until the same day, the exercise will still be of benefit.

## NEVER GO TO "AN AUDITION"

Never go to "an audition." Imagine instead, you're going to wherever your character would be going. Begin your involvement in the life of the character before you even leave home. Then the actual audition will be a continuation of the life you've already created.

As you dress for the audition, think about what your character wants and all the ways you are going to fight to get it. As you travel to the audition, fantasize about the obstacles in your way. Daydream about the character's hopes, fears, and secrets. Focus on the character's life, not the audition. Don't wait until you get there to begin this work. Getting lost in the life of the character is a lot more fun and helpful than focusing on the audition itself.

*Begin your involvement in the life of the character before you even leave home. Then the actual audition will be a continuation of the life you've already created.*

## GO TO A "FIESTA"

For some actors, the word "audition" has a negative connotation. It makes them feel as if they're taking an exam or getting called into the principal's office. As an actor you know how powerful words are, so rather than calling it an audition, why not relabel it a "fiesta?" It's hard to get nervous when you think you're about to attend a fiesta. It will remind you the whole thing is supposed to be fun.

# A COLD READING IS NOT
# A COLD READING

Don't be misled into believing that a cold reading is an exploration to give the casting people an idea of what you are capable of. Approach a cold reading as if it were a finished performance, not in terms of blocking, but in terms of the depth and specificity of your choices. You must come in prepared to do the performance you're going to deliver when they hire you.

## ARE YOU READY TO START AUDITIONING?

If you have a marketable look (young and gorgeous; an ethnicity that's in demand), your appearance may get you in the door, but if your work isn't up to par, this opportunity can backfire. If you read for a major TV or film project and you come across as awkward, nervous, or poorly prepared (or think you're doing brilliantly, but in actuality you don't have a clue), the casting director may be reluctant to bring you in for another project.

If you're not sure you're ready,* test the waters by submitting yourself for low budget independent projects, showcases, student films, and local theater. In these venues, you can make all the mistakes in the world and no one will remember.

*It should go without saying that you are participating in acting classes on an on-going basis.

*Auditioning for network television and major studio films is not an opportunity to practice your auditions skills. It's an opportunity to show the industry that you're ready to work <u>now</u>.*

## "BUT I DIDN'T HAVE ENOUGH
## TIME TO PREPARE"

The time you have to prepare will vary from audition to audition. In many cases, if you're working with an agent, you'll receive the material the night before. Occasionally, you'll have a few days to prepare, but it isn't unusual to get a call telling you to rush over to a casting office because you have an audition right now. It's your responsibility to do outstanding work, no matter how much time you have.

If you're uncomfortable working with little preparation time, take cold reading classes and join www.showfax.com. For approximately sixty dollars for the entire year, you can find material from almost every TV show and movie currently being cast. Download sides (audition scenes) from shows you think you'd be right for and give yourself varying amounts of time to prepare, e.g. fifteen minutes, thirty minutes, two hours, overnight. Invite a friend over and have her play the role of the casting director. Give her permission to read well or poorly. If you only have a few minutes to prepare, what you lack in time for specificity, you'll learn to make up for with spontaneity. You'll learn to trust your impulses, work moment to moment, and really listen. Soon it won't matter how much time they give you. You'll always be ready.

**Please note:** The more time you have to prepare, the more details and depth you can create for each of your answers to TEN MORE QUESTIONS TO ASK YOURSELF BEFORE EVERY AUDITION in this section.

***Don't wait until you have an audition to prepare for an audition.***

## PRE-PERFORMANCE RITUALS

If you were about to compete in the Olympics you would do everything in your power to put yourself in peak performance mode, knowing that the difference between winning a gold medal and finishing out of the running might be less than a split second. One of the things you would do would be to go through a checklist of pre-performance rituals; things you had done in the past to put yourself in the emotional and physical state you needed to be in right before your event. It's no different when you're auditioning. If you've done something in the past that created the conditions for you to do your best work, take the same steps every time you're preparing to read, e.g. breathing and stretching; giving your character a secret; doing a visualization; phoning a loved one for support; taking a hot bath; working with a coach; stretching and breathing; listening to a piece of music that puts you in the character's emotional state; doing a bunch of tongue twisters; singing scales to warm up vocally; getting a massage; praying; dancing; lip syncing to your favorite song; and arriving at the audition early so you have enough time to get centered.

**Note:** Pre-performance rituals are done in addition to the checklist of choices you make for your character. See TEN MORE QUESTIONS TO ASK YOURSELF BEFORE EVERY AUDITION in this section.

*If you've done something in the past that helped create the conditions for you to do your best work, take note of what it was so you can do it every time. That way doing your best won't be an accident, but an expectation.*

## THE CHARACTER'S NEEDS VS. THE ACTOR'S NEEDS

I once coached a wonderful actress who had been a series regular on a TV drama and was now auditioning for the part of a woman whose husband had just been shot. In the scene, her character is cradling and comforting her spouse as he lay dying in her arms. We spoke after the audition and I asked her how her reading had gone. She said she hadn't done very well because they didn't really know who she was, they had kept her waiting and they weren't very friendly. I asked her if those things were more important than comforting her husband as he lay dying. The point is, if you are fully involved in the character's given circumstances, you won't have time to worry about the things you can't control.

*The next time you have an audition, try the following experiment: pretend it's the other person's audition and you're there to make them look good. You'll get your attention off yourself and onto them, where it should have been in the first place.*

# ARE YOU SETTING THE BAR
# HIGH ENOUGH?

Many actors say to themselves, *"I don't care if I get the job. I only want them to like me"* or *"If I don't embarrass myself, I'll be happy."* Well, guess what? If that's all you ask for, that's probably all you'll get.

What do you think would happen if you said to yourself, *"I have something special to bring to this role"* and *"There's not an actor alive that can do this part as well as I can."?* You'd probably find a way to live up to your highest expectations rather than down to your smallest desires.

*Expect the most of yourself, rather than the least.*

# TRYING TO DO IT "THE RIGHT WAY"

Actors waste valuable preparation time trying to figure out "the right way" to do the role. Your choices must serve the material, but what you bring to it through your unique perspective, essence, and interpretation is something that can't be quantified as right or wrong.

The casting director may want to see you do it a different way, but that doesn't mean your way was the "wrong way." Art is created through the choices you make; it doesn't come down to right and wrong.

*Art is created through the choices you make; it doesn't come down to right and wrong.*

## "I DO GREAT WORK ONCE I'VE BEEN CAST, BUT I DON'T AUDITION WELL"

If you can use your imagination to believe you're a killer, a cop, a nurse or a politician, why can't you use your imagination to believe you've already gotten the part and you're on the set actually shooting? You go all out in acting class and you haven't been cast. Why not when you're auditioning? Holding back on an audition is like deciding you can't have fun on a date because you're not married yet.

*Gene Hackman has said that when he was first starting out he used to love to audition because it was often his only chance to actually play the part. This perspective enabled him to do his best work because he was no longer waiting to get hired to show them what he could really do.*

## THEY KNOW WHO YOU ARE. DO YOU KNOW WHO THEY ARE?

When you go into read, they'll have your resume but you won't have theirs. Therefore, part of your preparation should be to research the people you're going to be auditioning for. Look on the internet for the filmography of the director (web site: www.imdb.com), as well as that of the producer and the casting people. Familiarity with their previous projects may help you to understand the style of acting they gravitate towards, as well as giving you a possible topic for conversation.

# THE SINGLE MOST IMPORTANT QUESTION TO ASK YOURSELF BEFORE EVERY AUDITION

What is the one thing I can bring to this role that no one else in the entire world can?.....................myself.

## TEN MORE QUESTIONS TO ASK YOURSELF BEFORE EVERY AUDITION

1. What's taking place in the scene?
   (Given Circumstances)
2. What do I want? (Goal/Super-Objective)
3. Who and what is keeping me from getting what I want?
   (Obstacles)
4. What steps will I take to get what I want? (Actions)
5. What is my relationship to the other characters in the scene?
6. Do the other characters help or hinder in my pursuit of what I want?
7. How does what happened before the scene impact me emotionally? (Prior Circumstances and Moment Before)
8. How does the place where the scene occurs affect me emotionally?
9. What is my secret or hidden agenda?
10. What statement or question can I write at the top of each scene and silently repeat three times that will immediately get me involved in the scene? e.g. *"How can I get you to love me?" "Please don't leave me." I'm going to hurt you." "How can I trust you?"*

## DRESSING FOR THE PART

Always ask yourself how your wardrobe choices can enhance who your character is and contribute to what she is fighting for. For example, if you're up for the part of an attorney, high heels can give you a sense of power, allowing you to intimidate or seduce the other characters. But, you mustn't allow your wardrobe selections to overshadow your work. If the character is a soldier, you don't need to dress in full army regalia. A solid colored button down shirt, khaki pants, and dark shoes will allow them to picture you in the role. If you overdo it, the casting director may think you are insulting his intelligence by assuming he has no imagination. On the other hand, if you are reading for the part of a business executive, don't go in wearing shorts and a tee shirt. A suit is appropriate. If you're up for the part of a hot, sexy character and you're not sure how far to go, ask your agent to find out or call the casting office yourself. The assistant who answers the phone will be able to give an idea of what they're looking for. It will be one less thing to leave to chance.

*Wardrobe is the one prop you can sneak into every audition.*

## LEAVING YOUR PROPS AT HOME

In the Los Angeles and New York markets, unless you are told otherwise, do not bring props. Making strong choices, connecting, and emoting are more than enough to be concerned about. The casting people assume when you get to the set, you'll know how to use the appropriate props.

# DURING THE AUDITION

## THE CASTING DIRECTOR'S OFFICE

If you really believe you're in the place where your character is about to commit murder, or you're in the hotel room where you and your lover secretly rendezvous, or you're on the witness stand being cross-examined, you won't have time to get caught up in the distracting aspects of the casting director's office.

Part of your daily work should be to sensorially* create a core group of places that you can conjure up quickly, e.g. a place that makes you feel safe and comfortable; a place that makes you feel trapped; a place that makes you feel sexy; a place that makes you feel lonely. You can create places from your imagination and/or your past. If you're very specific and detailed in your work, you'll soon learn to create whatever place you need almost instantaneously. Then, the next time you have an audition, you'll be able to bring the observer into the world of your character, rather than losing yourself in theirs.

*Sensorially-using all five of your senses (taste, touch, smell, sight, hearing).

*Your job is to bring the casting people into your character's world, not to lose yourself in theirs.*

## IF THEY KEEP YOU WAITING

Rather than losing your focus, getting angry, or gossiping with the other actors in the waiting room, use the extra time to go more deeply into the life of your character. Use the character checklist at the end of the ACTING TECHNIQUE section to stimulate and deepen your preparation. Fantasize about an aspect of the character's prior circumstances that you haven't already explored. For example, if the scene is about getting a divorce, you might fantasize about how much you loved your partner when you first met. Use the time they keep you waiting to add depth to your role, rather than as an excuse for not doing your best work.

*If they keep you waiting, think of it as good practice for when you're working on the set.*

## GETTING PSYCHED OUT BY OTHER ACTORS

While you're in the reception area waiting to read, you'll sometimes hear other actors talking about all the fantastic projects they've done recently or how they just came back from celebrating Christmas with Steven Spielberg in the Bahamas. Why are they bragging about their incredible lives, rather than preparing to read? Most likely, they're trying to psyche you out to compensate for their own insecurities. Their lives may be as wonderful as they say, but right now they're in exactly the same boat as you: waiting for a chance to show people what they can do.

# YOU'RE NOT THE CASTING DIRECTOR

*"That other actor is so much more the character than I am. I don't even know why my agent bothered submitting me." "That blonde is so much sexier than I am". "That tall skinny guy is perfect for the part."*

The good news is you're not the casting director. You're the actor. Stick to your own job. That's more than enough to focus your attention on. Remember, they've seen your headshot. They already think you fit their image of the character. If they didn't, they wouldn't have called you in first place. Don't try to control the game by rejecting yourself before anyone else even gets a look at you.

**Note one:** Some actors feel that if they don't have a chance at getting a part, they have nothing to lose by really going for it. If this helps you to do your best work, then it's fine to imagine yourself out of the running.

**Note two:** The part of the Fonz in "Happy Days" had been written for a big, macho "street smart" type, not a short, sophisticated "Ivy leaguer." Henry Winkler could have easily told the casting people he wasn't right for the part. Instead, by the sheer force of his strong choices, he went down in history as one of the most memorable TV characters of all time.

**Note three:** At the very least, if you're not right for the role, but you do a great reading, they'll remember you and call you back for something else.

## THE CASTING PEOPLE AREN'T DOING
## YOU A FAVOR

Many actors present themselves in an overly grateful, apologetic, or tentative manner. Through self-effacing remarks and/or body language, they communicate that they aren't really good enough or up to the challenge; that the casting people are making a mistake by seeing them. The casting people will pick up on that energy from the moment you enter the room. If you don't believe you deserve to be there, neither will they.

*The audition begins the moment you enter the room, not the moment you begin to read.*

## YOU AREN'T DOING THEM A FAVOR

Some actors communicate through body language and/or snide remarks that they are too good to read. If they ask to see your work, it means you haven't proven yourself to these particular people. A poor attitude will not help you get the part (unless the role being cast is that of an arrogant asshole). Instead of creating an adversarial relationship, look at the reading as an opportunity to demonstrate how talented you are and how easy you are to work with.

# MAKING EXCUSES

*"My car broke down." " I got caught in traffic." "I missed my train." "I had to pick up my kid from school." "I got lost." "I just got the material." "My agent forgot to fax the sides over to me." "I had to take my dog to the vet." "My agent gave me the wrong material." "I've been really sick with the flu." "I had to work really late last night."*

Those are all wonderful excuses, but guess what? No one cares. If you make excuses at the audition, they will assume you'll make excuses when you get the job. Television and film production are stressful enough. Don't add to the tension. Save the drama for the role.

*The three cardinal sins for actors: being desperate, dull, and late.*

# TO SHAKE OR NOT TO SHAKE

Shaking hands with one actor doesn't take much time, but shaking hands with dozens of actors every week does. In addition, the casting person may be concerned about germs. Also, a flesh and blood connection may shatter the illusion that they're watching a performance. Let them initiate the handshake. A little thing to you may be a big thing to someone else.

## PREPARING IN FRONT OF THE CASTING PEOPLE

If you think you can take sixty seconds to prepare in front of them, you're wrong. Even thirty seconds will seem interminable and you will have lost them before you even start. You must be ready to read as soon as you enter the room. If you need a moment to center in front of them that's fine, but that moment shouldn't take more than five seconds.

*Everyone wants to see the baby. No one wants to know about the labor pains.*

## WHEN THEY WANT TO TALK FIRST

The audition process is not only conducted to see how well you read, but how easy you are to work with. If the casting people want to have a conversation with you before you read, it means they already see something in you that they like. Take advantage of this time to relax and really connect with them as people, not just casting people.

**Note one:** In most cases, unless they initiate conversation, letting your work speak for itself is your best course of action.

**Note two:** If you're doing a highly emotional scene, you must be able to get back into character in a matter of seconds.
(see step ten in TEN MORE QUESTIONS TO ASK YOURSELF BEFORE EVERY AUDITION in this section.)

19

## SHOULD I SIT OR SHOULD I STAND?

Most of the time, casting people don't care whether you sit or stand. Occasionally, they state a preference and quite often the actor is thrown if she's only practiced sitting and she's asked to stand or visa versa. The simple solution is to rehearse both ways. Your energy level and body language will be altered by this adjustment, so you must be comfortable reading either way.

## IF THEY CHANGE THE ORDER

It isn't unusual for an actor to be given three or four scenes to prepare for an audition. The problem occurs when she arrives at the reading, only to be told that only scenes two and three or just number four is being read. In many cases the rhythm, energy, and flow the actor has built from working the scenes in chronological order is lost. To counteract this problem, your preparation should include running the audition material in various sequences until it doesn't matter which scenes you're asked to do, or in which order you're asked to do them.

**Note:** Make sure you have a "strong moment before" written down at the top of each scene, so you always know where your character is coming from.

## HOLDING THE AUDITION MATERIAL

Instead of whining about having to hold the audition material, think of the sides as a good friend you are allowed to bring into the casting session with you. You don't have to look at your friend if you don't need to, but he or she is a glance away, just in case.

Get in the habit of turning the pages of each scene as you work, even if you don't think you need to. That way if you forget a line or the casting director jumps ahead by mistake, your friend will be there to assist you.

Write a short statement in large letters at the top of each scene that you can look at right before you read. The statement can be an intention *(I'm going to wipe that smug look off your face)*, a moment before *(I just went skinny dipping)*, a secret *(I stole the money)*, a reminder*(breathe and have fun)*, or a question. *(How dare you cheat on me?)* You will immediately become connected and grounded, thus allowing your friend, "the sides" to support you in doing your best work.

**Note:** Many casting people and directors believe if you're not holding the material during your reading, you'll be locked into a finished performance and you won't be able to take their adjustments. In addition, the casting people may be concerned that if you forget your lines, you'll fall completely out of the scene.

## BURYING YOUR HEAD IN THE SCRIPT

TV and film auditions are about the connection between you and the person you're reading with, not the connection between you and the paper you're reading from. If they can't see your face and your eyes, you might as well be on the radio. One solution is to have as much of the material off-book (memorized) as possible. Memorization is a muscle just like any other that can be strengthened with daily practice.

If you get the material at the last minute and there's no time for you to learn your lines, you'll still need to get your eyes off the paper as much as possible. To gain confidence working this way, practice the following exercise: get two copies of a scene book and sit down opposite another actor. Pick out a scene and read it over silently. Then read it out loud three times, getting your eyes off the page and onto your partner as much as possible. (Move your thumb down the paper so you always know where you are.) Go on to the next scene, repeating the same process. In a few weeks you'll become extremely skilled at working this way.

**Note one:** Memorizing your lines means knowing them so well that you don't have to think about them. If you don't know them perfectly, you're better off using the sides (audition scenes) to support your connection to the reader.

**Note two:** For short sentences, your eyes should be completely off the paper, whether you've memorized the material or not. For longer speeches, your eyes should be off the page on the first and last lines, as well as for your most important moments, e.g. if you're telling the other character you're going to kill them or that you love them, your eyes can't be buried in the paper. In addition, you must maintain the same pace as you would if you had the material completely off-book (memorized) and were doing a finished performance.

*If the people you're reading for can't see your eyes, you might as well be on the radio.*

## STAGE DIRECTIONS

In most cases, stage directions should be treated as suggestions, not commands or obligations. If it says in parenthesis (Mary sighs) or (Chuck chuckles) or (Tammy looks away), nine out of ten actors will do those actions only at the exact places indicated in the script. Reacting the same way at the same point as each of the other auditioners will not make your work stand out. Give yourself the freedom to express your unique emotional reactions when you feel them. As long as your emotional behavior serves the material, it needn't always be choreographed by the script.

**Note:** If the dialogue or events of the scene specifically call for an emotion or action (the other character asks why you are crying), it is strongly suggested you fulfill that direction.

## WHEN THE CASTING DIRECTOR READS BADLY

One of the things actors worry about most is what to do if the casting director reads badly (without inflection, poor eye contact, rushing through the material). You can prepare for this contingency by rehearsing your auditions with another actor in the following way: have your partner read her lines as well as she can. Then have her say her lines without any inflection or eye contact. Then have her rush through the material. Keep repeating this process until you can imagine you're getting what you need, no matter how your partner reads.

Another way to approach this problem is to use what the casting person is not giving you as an obstacle your character must overcome. For example, if your character is supposed to be angry or frustrated, you can blame the reader through the author's words for not giving you what you need. If it's a love scene and the reader is avoiding eye contact, you can imagine he's shy and you're trying to draw him out. If you can remember that every scene is about getting something from the other character that is being withheld, you can turn this flaw in the audition process to your advantage.

*The quality of your work must be contingent upon your ability, not the reader's.*

## ROMANCING YOUR GRANDFATHER

You use your imagination to create the character you're playing. Why not use your imagination to endow the casting director with the qualities you need in order to believe he is the other character? If it's a love scene, perhaps the reader has beautiful eyes or a sweet sounding voice or maybe you can imagine the reader as the young person he once was. You must still connect with the actual person you're reading with, but you can choose to focus on what you imagine is most appealing, rather than most distracting.

## VIOLATING THE CASTING DIRECTOR'S PERSONAL SPACE

Don't kiss, kick, spit on, or even touch the casting director. If he's concerned about his personal safety, he won't be focusing on the quality of your work. If he can smell your breath, you're way too close. Don't touch the papers on his desk or move his office furniture. Spark his interest by connecting with him emotionally, not physically.

## RUSHING YOUR READING

When you rush, you don't give yourself the time to experience each moment. In addition, you communicate that you value the casting person's time more than your own and that you don't believe you deserve to be there.

*Your goal is to do your best work, not to get in and out as quickly as possible.*

## LETTING THEM RUSH YOU

The casting person can control the pace of her reading but not the pace of your response. Just because she's in a hurry, doesn't mean the character you're playing has to be.

## CLICKING INTO THE MATERIAL HALF-WAY THROUGH YOUR READING

It is your responsibility to be fully connected for the entire read. If you know you do your best work after running the scene three or four times, you must find a way to do so before the audition. It is not the casting director's responsibility to run it with you until you're "there."

Fax the sides to a buddy the night before and run the lines over the phone before you leave home or on your cell phone as you head to the audition. Tape record the other character's lines and cue yourself through the material three or four times. Get to the audition early and find someone in the waiting room who is reading for a different role, go out in the hall, and run both of your parts.

## WHEN THEY DON'T RESPOND THE WAY
## YOU HAD HOPED

You can't always gage your work by the response in the room. If it's a comedy and they laugh hysterically, that's obviously wonderful. But what if they've already seen the scene fifty times? Or, what if the casting got into a fender bender on the way to work? You can't let their response or lack of one determine the caliber of your work. Decide you're going to have a great time no matter what their reaction and you'll always please the most important person in the room: you.

### *It's your audition. You lead, they follow.*

## MIMING THE ACTION

Unless you are a master mime or there is something unique about the physicality of the scene*, don't mime the action. No one will be impressed watching you drink from an invisible cup or pretending to cut and chew invisible food. The casting people assume when you get to the set, you will be given real props to use.

*If you're supposed to be holding a gun, it's certainly o.k. to point your index finger. If you're talking on the phone, it's acceptable to pretend you're holding a phone.

## FUMBLING A LINE

Actors sometimes take themselves completely out of a scene if they accidentally change a word or fumble a line. Their faces turn red and they think they've ruined the entire reading. The fact of the matter is everyone makes mistakes and if you don't make a big deal out of it, neither will they. If you do stumble and it takes you out of the scene, ask them to give you the cue line again, but don't be overly apologetic.

*Be more concerned about your character's needs than saying every word perfectly.*

## AD-LIBBING

As a general rule, unless you are told otherwise, stick to the author's words as closely to verbatim as possible. If you paraphrase or change the words intentionally, they may think you don't like what they've written, or you're trying to show them up. Remember, your job is to provide the subtext, not the text.

**Note:** There's an exception to every rule. I have some students whose ad-libs have helped them book jobs. The casting people had heard the dialogue so many times that the actors' ad-libs brought a freshness to the material. If you going to take this approach, you can't be the least bit hesitant or apologetic. You must trust your impulses and go for it.

## ACTING BY YOURSELF (NOT LISTENING)

If you're just waiting for the reader to finish saying his lines so you can continue acting by yourself, the casting people will only be seeing a portion of your capabilities. Remember, you're not just acting when you're saying your own lines. You're also acting when you're listening and reacting to the other character.

## IF THEY RE-DIRECT YOU

If you're given a directorial adjustment after your reading, take it as a positive sign. They wouldn't waste their time re-directing you if they hadn't responded to something you were already bringing to the role. Even if you did a great reading, they may want to be sure that you can take an adjustment.

**Note:** If they don't re-direct you, it doesn't mean you didn't do great work.

*"Accept direction as evidence of your capacity to be flexible, not as a statement of your incompetence."*
**-Paula Rosenfeld**

## PRETENDING TO UNDERSTAND THEIR DIRECTION

Quite often actors will nod their heads as if they understand the adjustment being given, when in reality, they have no idea what is being asked of them. If you're confused, politely ask them to rephrase their direction.

*You can't give them what they want if you don't understand what they're asking for.*

## SECRETS FOR ONE AND TWO LINE ROLES

1. Approach these auditions with the same degree of enthusiasm and specificity as you would for larger roles. Create a strong sense of place, a specific moment before, and an objective appropriate to the material.
2. Relax. You don't need to hit them over the head with your choices or to steal focus from the main characters.
3. Be prepared to play your part with three distinct interpretations.
4. In most cases, you won't have the entire script beforehand so if you're not clear on what they're looking for, ask the casting director.
5. Getting cast in one or two line roles is an opportunity to get seen by and to develop relationships with the same people who can bring you in to read for larger roles in the future.
6. Once you've done a few of these roles and have developed some contacts, let your agent know that you'd like to be submitted for more substantial supporting parts.

# AFTER THE AUDITION

## LINGERING IN THE CASTING DIRECTOR'S OFFICE

If you dawdle in the casting director's office to find out how you did or when the callbacks are, you may destroy the positive impression you made during the reading. It's the agent's job to get feedback and find out if you're getting a callback. If you aren't given any adjustments after your reading, politely thank them for their time and leave. They will remember you as a professional who let the work speak for itself.

**Note:** Right after you leave, casting people occasionally decide they'd like to hear you read again. Walk slowly to the elevator so they can catch you.

## THINKING OF ALL THE BRILLIANT THINGS YOU SHOULD HAVE DONE

It isn't unusual for actors to think of everything they should have done after the reading is over. The reason this happens is because the actor is more concerned about winning the approval of the casting person than immersing himself in the character's given circumstances. If you recognize this behavior as a pattern in your auditions, you need to spend more time doing relaxation exercises, personalizing the material, and creating a strong moment before.

*Your primary focus of attention must be on your character's journey, not the approval of the casting people.*

## WAITING ON PINS AND NEEDLES FOR FEEDBACK

If you did a great read and you're physically right for the part, you'll often get a call back. That's the best feedback you can hope for. The feedback your agent receives after your audition may have limited value. The casting director may convey her opinion to her assistant who communicates it to your agent's assistant who tells your agent who finally tells you what they said a week after the audition. A lot may be lost in the translation.

Often the feedback will be general. *"Oh, she was so adorable, just not right for this." " Too green." "We decided to go a different way." "Too tall." "Too short." "Not funny enough." "He's still in the mix." "It's not going to go any further."*

Translate any negative feedback into something you can use to improve your work rather than using it as evidence that you've chosen the wrong profession. For example, if the feedback is, *"You were green,"* it may mean you seemed nervous or you made choices that weren't strong enough or you were forcing the emotion. In any case, it points out you need to work on your audition skills.

Whether you eventually receive feedback or not, it is suggested that immediately after the audition, you write down what you felt worked and what could have been stronger. Take what you discover from your own analysis to find areas you can focus on to strengthen your work. Save your notes in a journal so you can see if your perceptions prove accurate over time.

## MAKING CHANGES FOR THE CALLBACK

You're getting called back because your work and your appearance fit the casting person's conception of the character. Unless you are told otherwise, they should be the same for the callback.

**Note:** Write down what you wore at the first audition as well as any directorial notes you have been given by the casting people.

*Making the same choices for the callback doesn't mean you can just imitate what you did at the first reading. You still have to do a strong preparation, experience what the character is going through, work moment to moment, and trust your impulses.*

# AGENT AUDITIONS

## DO'S AND DON'TS

1. A scene will demonstrate your ability to create relationship, chemistry, and connection more effectively than a monologue (if you're given a choice).

2. Don't wait for an appointment to start searching for material. You should begin to compile a library of scenes that are age and type appropriate <u>now.</u>

3. Don't choose material they've seen a million times. If you choose a scene from any popular movie, they will compare your performance to one that is indelibly etched in their minds as "the right way to do it." They've seen the scene from "Good Will Hunting," where Skyler asks Will to move to California too many times. Either they will say you were too much like Matt Damon and Minnie Driver or not enough like them.

4. Don't pick a scene partner with whom you are in competition. Select someone of the opposite sex that will make you look good, not over-shadow you. Pick a solid actor to work with, but not the next Marlon Brando or Michelle Pfeiffer.

5. Don't choose material that requires a lot of props or an excessive amount of physical movement. Get in and out without making a mess.

6. Don't apologize for your work. *"I didn't have enough time to prepare." "I was really nervous."* They're not interested in excuses, only results.

7. Do pick material that is entertaining. Making them laugh is usually preferable to making them depressed.

8. Don't choose material that is too long. Three minutes is an appropriate length. Always leave them wanting more of you, not feeling

**33**

that they've had more than enough of you.

9. Do choose material in which you can show a range of emotion.

10. Do remember there are lots of agents. If this is the right one it will happen. Don't make any single meeting a matter of life and death.

11. Don't think the agent is doing you a favor considering you for representation. You must believe you can do as much for the agent as he can do for you.

12. Do audition even if you're not sure if you want them to represent you. You are under no obligation to sign. Use this meeting as a practice session so when the agent you do want comes along, you'll be ready.

## FACING THE "DREADED" MONOLOGUE

For some actors, the thought of doing a monologue is worse than a trip to the dentist for a root canal. The following "Q and A" will alter your perspective.

*Why do I procrastinate when it comes time to finding and preparing monologues?*

You procrastinate because you feel like you're going to be out there all alone, scrutinized like a bug under a microscope. Since you're the center of attention, you think it's all about you. You're forgetting that a monologue is still a scene, even though you have all of the lines. The audience's attention may be on you, but your focus must be on whomever you're talking to (even if they exist only in your imagination). If you're worried about how you're doing or concerned about being judged, you haven't made strong enough choices to involve yourself fully in the author's given circumstances.

The other reason you procrastinate is because you're settling

**34**

for material you don't really love. It would be like cooking a meal of spam and brussel sprouts with soy milk gravy and wondering why you're not really hungry. If you continue to search until you find a monologue that you can't wait to sink your teeth into, your desire to procrastinate will disappear.

### *Will I need to prepare monologues for TV and film auditions?*

Unlike theater auditions where monologues are the norm, TV and film auditions almost never require monologues. In just about every case, you'll be reading from the actual material being cast. On the other hand, when auditioning for agents and managers, it isn't unusual for them to request a single monologue or two contrasting pieces.

### *If I'm doing a monologue for an agent, can I play it directly to her?*

Ask the agent for her preference before you begin. She may feel self-conscious if you look at her while you're performing. It may be easier for her to assess your talent if your focus is elsewhere, e.g. a chair or the wall. Also, it may be to your advantage not to use her. What if the agent yawns or has a twitch in her eye? You'll often do better if you can create someone from your imagination so you can get the reaction you need to propel your work.

*It's hard enough to perform with someone. How do I imagine someone who isn't there?*

The mistake actors make is to practice their monologues by themselves. The best way to prepare is to rehearse with another actor as if you were readying a scene. Before you begin your piece, give the other actor permission to react to everything you're saying. Allow them to interrupt, shout at you, ignore you, get up and storm out, kiss your hand, laugh at you, and chase you around the room. Repeat this exercise several times until you're fully connected. Next, instruct them to just sit there, listen to your piece and react silently. Then have them wait outside while you do your monologue to the empty chair they were sitting in. Keep repeating the process until you can do your piece and actually experience this person even when they're not in the room. Then when it comes time to actually do your monologue, you'll be bringing the energy of your partner into the agent's office with you, and you'll be fully engaged.

*What kind of material should I choose if the agent requests a monologue?*

1. Select material appropriate to your age and type. That way the agent can see if the two of you are on the same page in terms of how you should be marketed.
2. If you are only asked to do one piece, choose material which allows for a wide range of emotion (ideally something with comedic and dramatic elements).
3. Pick material that moves you. If you're not passionate about your selections, they won't be either.

### *How do I find a monologue that fits these criteria?*

You use your imagination in the creation of your performance. Why not use your imagination in your selection of material? If you've exhausted your local drama book store of monologue compilation books, perhaps you have a favorite passage from a special book that you've always loved, or a song lyric, or a poem you can turn into a monologue. How about doing a sonnet with a Brooklyn accent? Or a monologue where you play several characters with different accents and distinct physicalities? Or a monologue written for someone of the opposite sex? Or how about writing your own monologue, tailor-made to your strengths?

### *I would love to write my own monologue, but what if I'm a terrible writer?*

Everyone has an anecdote or remembrance from his or her own life that always gets a strong response. Try turning it into a monologue. If you don't like writing, tape record and transcribe it. Or tell it to a friend who does write and have them tweak it. If you decide to do your own piece and they ask you what it's from, tell them it's from Best Stage Monologues of 1997. They don't need to know that you wrote it.

### *I used to get a great response from my monologue, but now it falls flat. Should I dump it?*

You may be "phoning it in," i.e. doing it by rote. You need to break your piece down from scratch, the same way you would if you were handed new material. In addition, you may be imagining the person you are talking to is your therapist or a close friend and your objective is to get them to listen and understand your situation. The problem is a friend or therapist is already predisposed to listening and understanding so there aren't enough obstacles for your character to overcome. Imagine you're speaking to someone who hates you or thinks you're a liar. That way you'll fight harder to overcome your obstacles and you'll bring your monologue back to life.

*I feel weird acting in someone's office.*

If you can use your imagination to create the person you're talking to, why not use your imagination to sensorially create the place where your character's life is unfolding?

*One more question. How long should my monologue be?*

Two to three minutes is more than enough time to show them what you can do.

# COMMERCIALS

## MORE THAN A NUMBERS GAME AND HAVING THE RIGHT LOOK

Getting cast in commercials may be partially a numbers game (obviously the more auditions you have, the better your odds) and having the right look (but remember, plenty of actors have the right look). So what is it about the minority of actors who book the majority of spots? What's their secret?

1. They create a sense of reality and believability for everything they say and do.
2. They don't judge themselves, the product, or the copy. They immerse themselves in the given circumstances, no matter how ridiculous they may appear to the outside world.
3. They know that in thirty seconds they have to make every single moment count.
4. If they flub a line or change a word during the audition, they don't apologize or make a big deal out of it.
5. They're relaxed, believable, playful, and likeable.
6. If they need to be excited about the product but they're not, they imagine something else that does excite them.
7. They know that their non-verbal reactions are at least as important as any dialogue they have.
8. They imagine they're speaking to someone they care about rather than just a camera lens.
9. They know that doing commercials is a way to gain on-camera experience, exposure, membership in SAG, pay the rent, and to work with directors who may also shoot feature films.

10. They know that the slate (saying your name into the camera before reading the copy) is the actor's mini-commercial where they can show how warm, personable, and genuine they are.

**Note:** Some actors rush through the slate to get to the commercial copy, not realizing that the audition begins with the slate. In fact, when audition tapes are reviewed by the director and the client to decide who to call back, they may only look at the slate before fast forwarding to the next person.

*Your look may get you in the door, but it won't book you the spot.*

*Your slate must create an instant rapport that says you're happy to be there and ready to play.*

*More than fifty percent of all actors' income comes from commercials. If you don't want to do commercials, no one will force you. But, be aware of what you're giving up!*

# EXPECTING THE UNEXPECTED

## WHAT DO I DO WHEN............?

When you're dealing with casting people (and any other human beings) something unexpected always happens. You must be flexible and adapt quickly. Maintain a sense of humor and try not to take it personally.

The following are some of the things that might happen (but don't be surprised if what actually does happen isn't on this list):

1. Your agent said you were just reading for the casting director, but when you get in the room there are four producers, three writers, and the director waiting to see your brilliant work. Take a deep breath and focus on your character's objective.
2. You were told you were reading with Tom Hanks, but when you get in the room, only the casting director's assistant is there. Take a deep breath and focus on your character's objective.
3. You get completely new pages when you arrive. If you need some time to prepare, it's your responsibility to ask for it.
4. You were told to prepare scenes two and four, but they're doing scenes one and three. If you have all the sides in advance, be familiar with even the ones they said they definitely weren't doing.
5. They decide you aren't physically right for the part and they hand you new sides. Take the time you need to prepare in the waiting room.
6. You show up for the reading only to discover they forget to tell your agent the audition has been rescheduled or the part has already been cast. (Maintain your professionalism. Rant and rave to a stuffed animal when you get home.)
7. You were told it was just a meeting, but when you get there, they

hand you ten pages of material. Ask for some time to prepare.

8. They tape your audition after you were told they wouldn't be taping it. Keep your focus on the reader, not the camera (unless you're told otherwise).

9. The casting director reads one of your lines by mistake. Don't blame him. Just say *"I think we switched lines. Can we take it back a couple of lines."*

10. You read one of the casting directors lines by mistake. Ask to take it back a line. Do not be overly apologetic.

11. The casting director is reading all the other roles in the scene and decides to skip down and just give you your cue line. If you're thrown, politely ask to take it back a couple of lines.

12. As you enter the room, they let you know that the character is being done with a French accent. Even if you do one, ask if you can take a few minutes in the waiting room to make the adjustment. If you don't do one, tell them you would prefer to brush up on the accent and come back later.

13. The phone rings and the producer leaves to take an emergency call in the middle of your read. If you're thrown, ask if you can start over.

14. They eat lunch while you're reading. Keep your focus on your character's objective.

15. They call you in the second you get there. If you've arrived early and you need more time, let them know. If it's your appointed time, you must be ready to read.

16. They keep you waiting for two hours. (They get to run late. You don't.)

*Use the unexpected as an opportunity to make your work even more spontaneous and exciting.*

# SECTION TWO:
# THE BUSINESS

*"Whether you think you can or whether you think you can't............you are right."*
### -Henry Ford

*Is acting your career or your hobby?*

# DIVING IN

## YOUR ROAD MAP

Pursuing your career without a game plan is like taking a road trip without a map. You're certain to wind up somewhere, only it might not be where you wanted to go.

The first thing you need to do is write down your long term goals. Be very specific, e.g. the type of projects and material you ultimately want to be a part of; the range of characters you intend to play; the directors, writers, and actors you aim to work with; the managers and agents you want to represent you. (Read this list over every night right before you go to sleep, so your subconscious can align with your conscious effort to bring these goals to fruition.) Next, write down your intermediate goals, e.g. doing casting director workshops, networking, creating projects for yourself, finding an agent or a better agent. Next, write down your short term goals, e.g. taking acting and cold reading classes, learning dialects, getting a "kick ass" headshot, joining a theater company, submitting yourself for student and low budget independent film projects, earning your SAG card. Further refine your immediate goals into weekly and daily "to-do" lists that are within your control to achieve, e.g. you can't guarantee you'll get an agent within thirty days, but you can guarantee you'll send out your headshot/resume/cover letter to a specific number of agents and make follow up calls to each one.

*Once you know where you want to go, you can map out how you intend to get there.*

45

## THE PEOPLE WITH POWER

Most actors spend all of their time trying to win over casting directors and agents. Certainly that's important, but why not devote part of your time to developing relationships with the people who can actually hire you; producers and directors?

*"That's a great idea. But how do I do that?"* Make a list of ten films that you would love to have worked on and ten TV shows that you would be right for. Watch the credits at the beginning and the end of each of these projects to see who's responsible for their creation. Then begin a letter writing campaign. Tell these filmmakers how much you admire their work and be specific......that scene where so and so......the overall structure of the piece......Tell them about yourself and the work you are doing or you intend to be doing. Include a picture and resume. Write to people whose work you are genuinely passionate about. Don't make a pest of yourself, but write on a regular basis. A suggestion: don't target people as well known as Steven Spielberg. You want to concentrate on producers and directors who are not already pursued by every actor on the planet. Find the up-and-comers or the ones on the way down. You'll be surprised at what could happen. At the very least, they might pass your picture along to their casting director.

*Casting people and agents can only introduce you to the people who can hire you. Why not spend part of your time trying to meet the people who can actually give you a job?*

## GETTING IN THE DOOR WITHOUT ANY CONNECTIONS

There are several ways around the problem of not having any connections. If you work nights and weekends (to keep your days free for auditions), why not volunteer your services as an unpaid intern to a talent agent, casting director, producer, or director one day a week? Not only will you get in the door, but you'll see how the business really operates.

If your schedule doesn't permit one free day a week, why not do volunteer work at night or on weekends for an organization that is industry related? e.g. Women In Film or a prestigious film festival. You'll be helping two worthy causes: the organization and yourself.

If you have to work outside the acting profession to support yourself (and you live in Los Angeles), consider a job that can put you in proximity to the industry people you want to get to know, e.g. physical trainer, nanny, personal assistant, chef, masseuse, tutor, piano teacher, dog walker, house sitter, horse whisperer, karate instructor, tennis or golf pro. Once your industry connections get to know and like you, begin to put out subtle hints that you're also an actor. (If possible, let them think it's their idea to help you.)

*Developing contacts is as important as developing your talent.*

*Who you know is as important as what you know.*

## ASKING FOR HELP

Wanting to make it on your own is the rationale you may use for not asking for help, but in many cases there are deeper motives at play. What if you ask for help and the person says no? What if it makes them uncomfortable? What if they help you and you don't do well? If they do help, will you be obligated to give or do something in return?

The reality is no one does it alone. If you have connections in the business, but you're reluctant to call on them, you may need to change your perspective:

1. It's up to you to ask for what you need. It's not up to you to conclude how the other person is going to feel about your request. Assume they're adult enough to decide whether they want to help you or not.

2. You can only ask for help if you believe you have something of equal or greater value to offer in exchange; namely your talent.

3. If they want to help but don't know how, make your requests more specific. *"Could you introduce me to your casting person?" "Could you take my headshot up to your agency to see if they'd be interested in meeting with me?" "Can I show you my work?" "I know you're good friends with so and so. Could you inquire if they'd be willing to meet with me?"*

4. If your connection says he'll help, be sure to follow up (without being a pain in the ass).

5. Don't ask someone you hardly know for help. You must establish a relationship of trust and mutual respect before making your request.

6. Do not accept anyone's help if you must do something in exchange that will compromise your integrity.

*If you do ask for help, you're putting yourself on the line. If you don't ask for help, you're playing it safe. Which path do you think is more likely to get you what you want?*

## THE BUDDY SYSTEM

The acting profession is one of the most challenging in the world. Sometimes it's hard to stay motivated, particularly when you feel like you're out there on your own, without any support.

The solution is to set up a buddy system with another actor to make sure you stay on track. Implement the following steps to maximize the benefits of this process:

1. Meet with your buddy on a weekly, bi-weekly or monthly basis to establish goals and step by step "to-do" lists.
2. Establish a system of rewards and punishments to keep each of you motivated. *"If I don't keep my agreement to exercise every other day, I'll clean your apartment every week for a month." "If I practice my cold readings a half hour every day, on Saturday I'll reward myself by eating out and going to a movie."*
3. Check in with your buddy on a daily basis through e-mail or by telephone to make sure each of you is on track; let him know what you've accomplished and make sure he's doing what he said he would.
4. Celebrate victories and brainstorm new approaches for any setbacks.
5. If your buddy turns out to be a flake or doesn't press you to keep your agreements, find a new partner.

# THE NITTY GRITTY

## HEADSHOTS: THE GOOD, THE BAD, AND THE UGLY

If your photo is only "o.k." or "pretty good" or "not bad," you're wasting your time and money even mailing it out. If your photo doesn't look the way you actually appear in person, it's not going to help you. If your headshot doesn't capture your energy and your essence, it will not stand out. The key is in your eyes. They must communicate that you know who you are. In addition, your hair, clothing, and make-up must be congruent with an accurate assessment of how you're going to be sold to the industry. (If you're not sure how to market yourself, do the exercise from TYPECASTING in this section.)

## THE PRACTICE ROUND:

Have a friend take several shots of you. (You can even use a disposable camera.) You're not going to actually use these shots, but they will give you a good idea of what works best for you. Relax. Play. Experiment. As you look in the camera lens, imagine different people gazing back at you: someone who makes you feel sexy; someone who loves you; someone who makes you laugh. Using all five of your senses, imagine you're somewhere that puts you in a positive emotional state: a balmy tropical oasis; a mountain retreat in front of a crackling fireplace; a football field; on a shopping spree at your favorite clothing store. Silently run the words of a monologue or recall the lyrics of a song that really move you. Imagine your favorite smells: freshly baked bread; apple pie; the scent of roses. Bring along a portable C.D. player, blast your favorite music, and dance around between shots. Close your eyes and think of a secret that makes you feel sexy, wonderful, or naughty. As soon as you open your eyes, have your friend snap the shot. See what happens if you take a few deep breaths and do nothing but relax while you're being photographed. Be sure to try several changes of clothing. When you get these shots back, you'll be able to see if you're projecting too much or too little, and if your hair, clothes, and make-up, enhance or detract from what you're trying to communicate. This practice round will wind up saving you several hundred dollars, a lot of time, and a great deal of frustration.

## INTERVIEWING PHOTOGRAPHERS:

Interview at least five photographers so you have a basis for comparison. Bring the shots from your practice round as well as old headshots from previous shoots. Get the photographers' opinions on how they would sell you; the type of clothing they would suggest to enhance, but not overshadow what you're trying to convey. Study their sample book of headshots. Some photographers do better work with men than women and visa versa. Some do better with character actors, some with leading types. Make sure the background in the photos doesn't distract from the faces. Notice if the actors are posing in ways that look phony or awkward, e.g. chin leaning on the hands; forced smiles. Find out the fee for re-shoots in case you're not happy with your shots. It should be minimal. Find out the additional cost for a hair and make-up person. Get everything in writing. Your goal is to find someone you feel comfortable with, someone whose work you love, and someone who's affordable. Remember, you're buying their services. If you feel intimidated or put off by a photographer, no matter their reputation, go somewhere else.

**Note:** Consider bringing "tear sheets" from magazine ads and layouts. You don't want your shots to appear "modelly," but there may be a look or style that shows what you're going for.


## THE NIGHT BEFORE THE SHOOT:

Do the following visualization exercise ten minutes before you go to sleep: close your eyes and imagine you're at the shoot. See yourself as relaxed, playful, and confident. Imagine the camera is the sun and you're basking in its warmth. You have a wonderful connection and rapport with the photographer. You're having more fun than you've ever had in your life. You're surprised at how much you enjoy getting your picture taken! You feel alive, vibrant, and excited, yet at the same time completely at ease. Now take the visualization further: a few days have passed and you get your photos back. Not only do you love them, but everyone else who sees them acknowledges how wonderful they are and that they truly capture your essence. While you're asleep, your subconscious will work on creating these results. Make sure you get plenty of rest.


## THE SHOOT:

As you did in the practice round, bring music that puts you in different moods; upbeat, reflective, sad, powerful, sexy, friendly, warm. If it helps you to relax, bring a friend or lover to the shoot. Rather than thinking of it as a photo shoot, imagine you're hanging out with friends with whom you can truly be yourself. Whatever relaxation exercises you do to prepare for an audition, do for the shoot. Do whatever worked in the practice round so you're not doing too much or too little.

## JUDGEMENT DAY:

When you get your contact sheets (thumbnail sized prints of each shot), show them to lots of people. You are looking for a consensus of opinion. Seven out of ten people should agree on the same shots as being outstanding. Next blow up all the shots you think might work to 4" by 6" and show them again. Continue to narrow down your choices. Get more opinions. When it comes to photos, they must please your intended audience even more than they please you. Of course, if a picture makes you feel bad about yourself, no matter how many people like it, don't use it. Next blow up the shots that get the best response to 8" by 10" and narrow your choices further. If you get two great headshots (ideally one light and playful, one dramatic), you've done well. If you're not happy, don't be discouraged. Re-shoot or find another photographer. Rome wasn't built in a day.

***You must know how you're going to be sold to the industry <u>before</u> you get your headshot taken.***

***The key to a great headshot is in your eyes. They must communicate that you know who you are.***

# YOUR RESUME

Think of your primary promotional tool (photo and resume) as if it were a new brand of cereal. As we scour the supermarket shelves, the first thing we notice is the front of the box: your photo. If it sparks our interest, we'll turn it around and check out the ingredients on the back: your resume. Your job is to make the ingredients sound as tasty as possible without getting sued for false advertising.

If you're just starting out, your headshot is likely to have much more impact than your resume, but that doesn't mean you can just write your name, phone number, height, and weight on a piece of paper, stick it on the back of your headshot and think that you're done. First of all, if you're sending out your photo/resume, it's because you're ready to work. Hopefully, it's not just a gut feeling, but based on concrete evidence. Perhaps you have some experience doing high school, college and/or local community theater. Maybe you've been part of a theater company or have acted in some student films or have worked on a show at your local public access cable station. At a minimum, you've taken technique, scene study, and cold reading classes.

On the following page is a sample resume of someone just starting out with notes and suggestions to follow:

# ELLIE MAY CLAMPETT

(310) 555-1255

EYES:BLUE          HAIR:BLONDE

## FILM AND TELEVISION

| DOG TOWN | LEAD | UNIVERSITY OF ARIZONA |
| WINDFALL | SUPPORTING | UNIVERSITY OF ARIZONA |
| THE BLUES | LEAD | CABLE-PHOENIX |
| KICKER | SUPPORTING | CABLE-PHONEIX |

## THEATRICAL AND REPRESENTATIVE ROLES

| HORROR TOWN | JUDY | LITTLE LAKE THEATER CO. |
| GLASS MENAGERIE | LAURA | BAKERTOWN PLAYERS |
| GETTING OUT | ARLENE | THE ACTORS SPACE |
| THE WAGER | HONOR | NEW WEST THEATER CO. |
| ENTER LAUGHING | WANDA | NEW WEST THEATER CO. |
| FOUND A PEANUT | JOANIE | THE ACTORS SPACE |
| TORCH TOWN | MELANIE | THE ACTORS SPACE |
| THE BOYFRIEND | POLLY | THE ACTORS SPACE |
| MUSIC MAN | MARIANNE | THE ACTORS SPACE |

## COMMERCIALS &INDUSTRIALS   CONFLICTS AVAILABLE UPON REQUEST

## TRAINING
SANDRA CORELY-CAMERA TECHNIQUE
ROCKLAND INSTITUTE- TECHNIQUE, SCENE STUDY
BRIAN ANDREWS-COLD READING, SCENE STUDY
ANDREA ROCKLAND-IMPROVISATION

**SPECIAL SKILLS:** scuba certification, yoga instructor, pilot's license, black belt karate, sign language, pool shark, ice hockey. Accents: French, Russian, Italian.

1. Neatness and spelling count.

2. A voice mail contact number is sufficient. Exclude your age, home phone number, address, and social security number.

3. Suggestion: <u>exclude</u> your height and weight (unless you're a "super-model" or a "Mr. Universe" type). It may keep them from bringing you in on a project, for which you would otherwise be perfect.

4. If you are listing school productions, write the name of the theater rather than the name of the school, unless it's a prestigious performing arts high school or college.

5. If you haven't done any full scale productions, write down scenes you've done in class under representative roles.

6. If you were an extra, do not upgrade yourself to a principal role. You will be found out. Extra work should be excluded from your resume.

7. Do not list specific commercials you've shot. The casting director will assume these commercials are still airing and will not bring you in for competing products.

8. Technique, scene study, improvisation, commercial, and cold reading classes are important, but you don't need to include every single class you've ever taken.

9. Include any special skills for which you have exceptional ability. Exclude anything that you sort of do, e.g. ordering enchiladas in a Mexican restaurant does not mean your special skills include fluency in Spanish.

10. Be able to speak articulately and confidently about everything on your resume.

*Don't ever apologize for what's not on your resume. Make the most of what is there.*

## THE CARE AND FEEDING OF AGENTS

*What's the best way to get an agent?*

Approach everyone you know who has representation and ask them to take your headshot/resume to see if they can set up a meeting for you. If you just mail in your headshot with a cover letter mentioning your mutual connection, it may get lost in the shuffle. The person who already has the relationship should always make the inquiry.

If you don't have any connections, target thirty agents who you'd like to work with. Send your headshot with cover letters and follow-up postcards, letting each of them know what you're working on. Keep track of when these agents are attending industry workshops and showcase your work until they either bring you in for a meeting or make it clear that they're not interested. Intern* one day a week for one of your targeted agents so they can get to know you on a personal level. If you get a part on your own, call one of these agents and ask them to negotiate the contract. If you know a casting director who really likes your work, have him call a few of these agents on your behalf.

*Volunteer to answer phones and file. Tell them you want to learn about the business from the inside.

*Do I really need to include a cover letter when I mail my picture and resume to an agent?*

Even though your picture and resume are likely to have much more impact, always include a brief cover letter, if for no other reason than to be polite and professional. The cover letter basically states you're seeking representation and would love to set up a meeting. If you're working on a project, know someone they're already representing, getting auditions and callbacks on your own, hail from the same hometown, or attended the same college, that information should certainly be prominent in your letter. If you're a creative writer and/or have a good sense of humor, incorporate that into your brief communication.

**Note:** Your envelope is more likely to be opened if you address it to a specific agent rather than just the agency itself.

### How do I tell what kind of reputation an agency has?

Call a few casting offices and ask if they know and work with the agency you're interested in. You needn't speak to the actual casting director or even give your name. The assistant who answers the phone will know the answer and in most cases, give you their impressions. In addition, ask your fellow actors what they've heard.

If you get a meeting, note your first impressions. Does everyone seem to be focused, professional, and organized? Is the agency located in a nice part of town? Is the office well decorated or cheaply furnished? Are the phones ringing off the hook? Ask who some of their working clients are. The more successful the clientele, the easier it will be for them to get you seen.

### I've been offered to sign with a newly established agency. I really like them a lot, but I'm not sure how much they can get me out.

New agencies pop up all the time. They might be terrific, but you need to do some research. Find out if they're a spin-off or a consolidation of two or more established agencies. If so, they may have the industry connections to get you in the door. On the other hand, if you discover no one knows them, it may be difficult for them to set up meetings. This factor should not preclude representation, but it certainly must be considered. Their enthusiasm and drive may compensate for a lack of connections.

***Should I even bother pursuing the top agencies?***

The advantage of a top agency is that they have the clout to get you seen for just about everything they submit you for. The disadvantage is that since the top agencies handle stars, most of their work consists of fielding offers, rather than submitting and promoting newer talent. In most cases, they won't be hungry enough to put in the time and effort to get you out there because their financial return won't be great enough. If you're just starting out, you'd be better off focusing on smaller and mid-sized agencies that have the ability and desire to get you seen for co-star, day player, and guest star roles. Once you've developed a body of work, you can move up the scale to the bigger agencies who have access to the more prestigious, star driven vehicles.

**Note:** If you do get the opportunity to work with a top agency when you're just starting out (you might have an extremely marketable look or an industry connection), it will be your responsibility to avoid getting lost in the shuffle. One way to accomplish this is to develop a strong relationship with your primary agent's assistant. This is the person to whom you'll have ready access and who has your agent's ear.

***What if I sign with an agent, but she doesn't get me out enough? Am I stuck for the length of the contract?***

According to the Screen Actors Guild, if you don't get work within any 91 day period you can sever the agent/client relationship, no matter how much time is left on the contract.

*I met an agent who wants to work with me, but insists I use the photographer and the acting teacher he recommends.*

If their recommendations are a requirement for representation, they're making the bulk of their money from kick-backs. This is not an agency you want to work with. Move on.

*I met with an agent who wants me to pay a monthly fee to cover the cost of phone calls and mailings on my behalf.*

A franchised agent receives a 10% commission for work procured. There are no other legitimate fees to be paid by the actor.

*An agency has asked me to sign across the board. First of all, what does that mean and secondly, is that a good thing?*

Signing across the board means you're going to be working with the agency's theatrical department (TV and film), as well as the commercial department, and in some cases the print department. Before you sign on the dotted line, research the extent of the agency's connections in each of these venues. Some full service agencies make almost all of their money from commercials and have limited TV and film access.

**Note:** If you're just starting out, consider working with an across the board agency, even if their connections are primarily in the commercial arena. It's still a good chance to get your feet wet.

*I met with an agency that wants to work with me commercially, but not theatrically.*

They may want someone with more credits or they may already have someone in your category. If you like the agency, work with them commercially, while you do everything you can to change their minds. At the same time, continue to pursue theatrical representation elsewhere.

**Note:** see AGENT AUDITIONS: DO'S AND DON'TS in the AUDITIONS section.

*Hallelujah! I finally have an agent! My worries are over.*

Actors often believe that once they've signed with an agent they're home free. The phone is going to ring off the wall and all of their needs are going to be taken care of. Certainly an agent can make a major difference in an actor's career, but getting an agent is not equivalent to finding the holy grail. Even with an agent, some actors sit around for months without a single audition. On the other hand, there are actors who work all the time, even though they don't even have agents. The bottom line is, your career will never cease to be your responsibility, whether you have an agent or not.

*How can I stay on top of my agent without making a pest out of myself?*

When you sign with your agent, ask her the best way for you to keep in touch. Is it o.k. to check in every week or once a month by phone or in person? Send postcards? Let her know who you're meeting at industry showcases? Call her when you hear about a part you might be right for? Call her after an audition to let her know how you did? Invite her to see you in a play? Take her out to lunch? In addition, whenever your agent calls you with an audition, consider picking up the material at her office rather than having it faxed to your home. That way if there are other agents in the office, they'll get a visual reminder that you're out there.

*Like everything else in life, there's a proper balance. You don't want to become a pain in the ass, but you also don't want to disappear from the agent's mind without a trace.*

*I'm working harder on my career than my agent is. I'm getting auditions and booking jobs on my own. Why should I even have to give her 10%?*

If you're getting auditions and landing roles on your own, congratulations! It means you're taking control of and responsibility for your career. Plus, now you have leverage. If your agent doesn't start to earn her 10% by taking advantage of the fact that you're never in more demand than when you're already working, your new agent will.

*I know I'm being submitted, but I'm not getting any auditions.*

It isn't unheard of for an agency to send out fifty or more copies of an actor's headshot every single month. It's likely the agent is submitting the actor for every role for which she is even remotely castable. What's wrong with that? Nothing, except that being submitted is not the same as being seen. Whether you actually get in the door to read depends on whether the casting

**62**

people even open the envelope containing your agent's submission. Casting people have relationships with certain agents with whom they've built a rapport over the years. One of the determining factors for that rapport is the quality of talent the agency has submitted in the past, i.e. does your agent have a reputation for submitting talent that consistently does outstanding work?

*My agent sent me out on a flurry of auditions when we first started working together, but I haven't heard from her in months. It's like I've disappeared from the face of the earth.*

You're being warehoused. She put you out on the display floor but you didn't sell so she stuck you on a shelf in the back room. Set up a meeting and ask her what you can do to revive her interest. If you can't rekindle her enthusiasm, look for a new agent. (If someone requests you for an audition or offers you a role, she'll most likely become interested again.)

*Three months ago I got new headshots at my agent's request. He seemed to love the shots, but he's already asking me to get new ones.*

It isn't unusual for an agent to tell you that your headshot isn't pulling (getting you meetings), but what he won't tell you is that he doesn't have the clout to get you in the door. Rather than rushing out to get new headshots every three months, ask five industry people what they think of your current photos. If they all agree that they're fantastic, you might consider looking for a new agent instead of a new photographer.

*My agent gets me in on everything I'm right for, but I get the sense that casting people don't really like him. Should I try to find someone nicer?*

The agent represents you, not the casting person. Being nice is not a requirement. A good agent knows when to turn on the charm and when to "bust balls." The bottom line is, if you're getting in to read and you're not losing roles because your agent is asking for too much money, he's doing his job.

*My agent gets me in on a lot of roles I have no interest in playing.*

Your agent is submitting you for the parts she thinks you're right for and has the connections to get you in on. If you're unhappy with how she sees you, set up a meeting and let her know what you will and won't do. But, be aware that if you set too many restrictions, your agent may decide you're not worth the time and effort and suggest you go somewhere else.

*I have a big audition coming up. I don't care whether I get the part. I just want my agent to get good feedback so she'll believe in me.*

If your agent didn't think you were talented, capable of doing good work, and actually getting the part, she wouldn't have submitted you in the first place. So if your major concern is winning her approval, you're focusing on what you've already achieved. Shift your attention to something a lot more relevant and a hell of a lot more fun: total immersion in your character's given circumstances. Remember, if you're doing the work, you won't have time to focus on things you can't control, like opinions and feedback.

*Every time I speak to my agent my palms sweat. I guess he makes me nervous.*

If your palms are sweating, it's because you are laboring under the misconception that the agent can do more for you than you can do for him; that somehow he is doing you a favor by representing you. If you truly believe that, why not make a deal with your agent? Tell him you'll take 10% and he can keep 90% of everything you make. Your agent might be happy, but he would certainly question your sanity because he knows that the percentages are the way they should be. He knows that when people go to the movies or watch TV they're not thinking, *"Hey! Where's Julia Robert's agent? That's whose work I really want to watch,"* or *"Gosh! Why don't they put Brad Pitt's agent on the cover of People Magazine? That's whose face I really want to see."* The reason you get to keep most of the money is because you're the one everyone is interested in. Remember, without you, your agent has nothing to sell. If anyone's palms should be sweating, it's his.

*There are lots of agents out there. There's only one of you.*

*If your agent didn't believe you could do as much for him as he can do for you, he wouldn't be representing you.*

*Your agent works for you. You don't work for him.*

*How come my agent always seems so abrupt and harried?*

The reality is, like everyone else in the business, your agent is operating without much power and control. For example, an agent may discover someone he thinks is fantastically talented, introduce him to every one in town, only to have that actor get snatched up by a bigger agency. When Cuba Gooding, Jr. won the Academy Award for "Jerry McGuire" he thanked Coralie Jr., the agency that first took a chance on him. He wasn't even with that agency anymore. James Woods' agent sold his own car to pay for Woods' screen test for "The Onion Fields" because the producers didn't want to spend the money. James Woods, not only got the role, but it made his whole career. He is no longer with that agency.

An agent may devote a year or more to promoting an actor he believes in without ever making a cent. The agent has to pay rent and overhead, whether the actor gets work or not.

Imagine how frustrating it is to believe in an actor and not be able to get him seen because the casting people don't think the actor is quite right for the part. If you hate hearing the word "no," think of how an agent must feel. They hear "no" hundreds of times a day.

You may know how hard it is to think you've landed a role only to hear that it went to someone else. Imagine having to deal with that situation everyday.

If an actor is late, rude, or unprepared, that reflects back on the agency and makes it that much harder for the agent to get his other clients into read.

In the past, a well established actor who may have received hundreds of thousands of dollars for each project is now receiving "take it or leave it" offers of scale plus ten*. There's money for the star and no one else. Who do you think that actor is going to blame and leave?

No one wants or deserves to be treated rudely, but if you take a moment to see the business through your agent's eyes, you'll realize that your agent is in the same boat as everyone else.

*Screen Actors Guild minimum plus ten percent more for the agent.

*Take a moment to look at the business from your agent's point of view and you might not take his behavior so personally.*

*I want to leave my agent. Should I fire my old agent now or wait until get a new one?*

If you like your agent, but she doesn't get you out enough, fire her after you find your next agent. In most instances, it's better to have an agent than no agent.

On the other hand, if you really can't stand being associated with your current agent because she's sleazy, lazy, negative, or dishonest, fire her first. This is not someone you want on your team for even another minute.

*I'd like to go to a better agency but I'm really close to my current agents and I don't want to hurt their feelings.*

Your loyalty is admirable, but you're forgetting that this is a business.Meet with your agents on a regular basis to make sure you're both doing everything possible to get you out there. That way you won't feel guilty, and they won't be shocked, if and when you do leave.

# MANAGERS: TO HAVE OR NOT TO HAVE?

1. Some actors believe they only need a manager when they're established and already have a career to manage. The reality is there are many managers who will help to develop undiscovered talent. At every stage of the game you want to at least investigate having any reputable person on your team who can assist you in procuring work.

2. An agent may have a hundred or more clients, whereas a manager will only represent ten or fifteen actors. A manager will be able to give you and your career a lot more individual attention.

3. A good manager will be able to set you up with a good agent or be able to get you auditions without an agent. (Managers aren't supposed to submit you for parts, but this rule is rarely enforced.)

4. A very good manager will be able to introduce you to casting people, directors, and producers on a regular basis.

5. A great manager will create and produce projects in which you can appear.

6. Before signing with a manager, research her reputation, clout and connections in the same manner you would for an agency (see THE CARE AND FEEDING OF AGENTS in this section).

7. If you're working with an agent you like and you're thinking of signing with a manager, discuss it with your agent first. You want your team to work together harmoniously and some agents may feel resentful if you spring a manager on them without first getting their input.

8. Some managers attempt to eliminate direct contact between agent and actor, preferring all communication be handled through the manager. Don't go along with this. Maintain a relationship with anyone and everyone involved in your career on a regular basis.

9. Occasionally agents and managers bad mouth each other as they compete for your loyalty. If you find this to be the case, set up a meeting to see what each of them needs to do to benefit your career without stepping on each other's toes.

10. Before signing a management contract, review it with an attorney. Discuss removing items that don't serve you and adding things you need for your protection, e.g. a clause that allows the contract to be terminated if either party is dissatisfied; the percentage of commercial residuals the manager will receive if she is not actively involved in procuring commercial work. Unlike contracts between actors and SAG franchised agents, there is no governing body for managers, so the specifics of the individual contract are very important.

11. Unlike a SAG franchised agent who is only entitled to ten percent of your earnings, a manager may want ten, fifteen, twenty or even twenty-five per cent. Ten to fifteen percent is the industry standard and should be the maximum.

12. Some managers may want you to contribute to the cost of submissions and phone calls until you start earning money. If a manager won't cover this financial investment, she doesn't belong on your team.

13. Standard managerial contracts state that the job of a manager is to provide advice and guidance. But remember, all the advice and guidance in the world isn't worth very much if it doesn't lead to work.

*Actors are sometimes surprised and resentful that managers, like agents, get their percentages whether they actually help you get the job or not. It's up to you to see that your manager is earning her commissions, if not directly, then through advice, support, and connections.*

# AGE OLD QUESTIONS

## WHAT TO SAY WHEN YOU HAVE NOTHING TO SAY

If a director or producer decides to hire you, you're going to be spending anywhere from one day to several months working together. An interview can help them to see that you're pleasant, friendly, and fun to be around. Before an agent agrees to represent you, they'll want to get a sense of who you are and what you're about.

*"But I don't know what to talk about."* It doesn't matter what you talk about as much as how you talk about it. You can talk about baseball, cooking, current events, their office decor, your goldfish, performances you've seen, parts you've done or would like to do. Communicate with passion and humor. Be genuine. You are looking to engage them in conversation so they can get to know, like, and trust you. Perhaps you have something in common. Your conversation is a dialogue, not a monologue. You needn't do all the talking.

*"I'm great once I have the material but I'm very shy personally and don't like to talk about myself."* Fine. You're an actor. Create a character who likes to talk about himself and has a lot to say. If you can play a killer, you certainly should be able to play someone who's warm, friendly, and engaging. Role-play mock interviews with your fellow actors until you're comfortable.

*An interview is an indication of their interest, not a challenge or a test. If you don't like to talk about yourself, create a character who does. If you can play a killer, you certainly should be able to play someone who's warm, friendly and engaging.*

**70**

## PAID SHOWCASES: YEA OR NAY?

1. Years ago, casting people and agents scoured local theater looking for new talent. Today, they're being paid to attend showcases so they're less likely to see you in a play or an evening of scenes (if all you're offering is wine and cheese). If a play has gotten great reviews, has a big name in it, or is in a prestigious theater, they still might attend without payment.

2. It may seem that casting people are primarily there to pick up a check, but if you do fantastic work and stay in touch (through postcards and photo/resume updates) and there's a role being cast for which you're right, there's a good chance you'll get called in to read.

3. If you do get called in from a showcase, it will usually be to read for the smaller roles.

4. Doing showcases is a good way to get in the game if you're just starting out, or to get back in the game if you've been away for awhile.

5. Showcasing is an opportunity to practice your audition skills so when you do have an actual audition you'll be ready.

6. Showcasing is not a place to learn how to act but to improve upon what you already know how to do.

7. It's a way to get to know what they're looking for and to make choices quickly.

8. If you do poorly, you can do another showcase for the same people next month and show them how brilliant you really are.

9. If there's a particular TV show that you dream of working on, showcasing is an opportunity to get seen by the people who cast that show.

10. Showcase disclaimers state that they don't guarantee employment but are educational tools. Use them as such. If something isn't clear, ask. There are no stupid questions.

11. If you resent doing showcases on the principle that it's wrong to pay to show your work, don't do them. A bad attitude won't help you.

12. Casting directors will be providing material from projects that have already been shot so your choices will be compared to those of the hired actors. Therefore, take their critiques with a grain of salt. Just because you made different choices doesn't mean your choices were wrong. Don't argue. Just show them how easily you can take their adjustments.

13. In most cases, if you're not in the Screen Actors Guild, you'd be better off waiting until you get your membership card to do showcases. The casting people will be much more likely to call you in.

14. If you have an agent, see how she feels about paid showcases before you sign up. Some agents are enthusiastic because it makes their job easier. Others feel they have the clout to get you in on everything you're right for without showcases.

*It's fine if you don't want to do paid showcases. What are you willing to do instead that will yield equal or greater results?*

## YOU'RE ONLY AS OLD AS YOU LOOK

Telling people in the industry how old you really are is like telling them how much money you have in the bank. It's none of their business. The only thing that matters is how old you appear to be. If the role calls for a twenty year old and you look that age, there is no reason to tell them you're really twenty eight.

1. If you're asked how old you are, state the age you've chosen as the simple truth. Don't say, *"How old do you think I am?"* or *"I don't tell people my age."* They'll study your face until they decide you're the wrong age for the part.
2. Ask everyone you meet how old they think you are (except the people you're auditioning for). The age you hear most often is the age you should use.
3. If it violates your integrity to lie about your age, don't do it.
4. If you look your real age, there's no reason to lie.
5. If you look older than your real age, it's better to use the age you appear to be.
6. If you look eighteen, but as soon as you open your mouth you seem a lot more mature, create a character that speaks, moves, and thinks like an eighteen year old. You must be able to convey age appropriate behavior from the moment you enter the room.
7. If the casting person pulls you aside and says, "Just between you and me, how old are you really?" stick to the age that got you the audition. Telling them the truth won't help you get the part.

*If you went up for the part of a character of Greek heritage, would you feel obligated to tell them you were really Italian? Of course not! So why would you feel obligated to tell them your real age?*

# TYPECASTING

*"I can play anything. I get so frustrated when they only see me one way."*

When you're starting out, you should be able to play roles based on your physical appearance, even if they're not representative of your self-image and background. For example, if you grew up in Beverly Hills and you got your masters degree from Harvard, but you look like a Mafia hitman or a gang banger, you must be able to pull off the body language and dialect for these type of characters. If you're Israeli or Italian, but everyone thinks you're Cuban, it would be in your best interest to perfect a Cuban accent and even learn to speak Spanish. If you're a genius, but you look like Marilyn Monroe, you should be able to make us believe you're a ditzy blonde. The reason is, when you appear on camera, the audience automatically makes assumptions about you. If your performance is inconsistent with your physicality, it takes them out of the story. Agents and casting people operate the same way. They assess who and what you are the moment they meet you. It will make your life easier if you can give them what they expect.

If you're not sure where you fit in, try the following exercise: go to the shopping mall with a friend. Stand in one spot without speaking and have your friend approach shoppers one at a time, point to you and ask them to take a thirty second survey. You can cull your questions from this list or make up your own.

1. Do they think you look like a hero/heroine/villain/victim?
2. White collar/blue collar/bum?
3. Cop/crook/judge/attorney?
4. Doctor/nurse/patient?

5. Kindergarten teacher/college professor/high school or college student/drop-out/slacker?

6. Would they expect to see you on a soap opera/sitcom/nighttime drama?

7. How old do they think you are?

8. Wealthy/middle class/poor?

9. Ethnicity/religion?

10. Funny/serious?

11. Successful with the opposite sex?

12. Lecherous/monogamous?

13. Bossy/wishy-washy?

14. Athletic/couch potato?

15. Warm and loving/someone to avoid in a dark alley?

16. Life of the party/wallflower?

17. Would they expect to find you at McDonalds or a fancy French restaurant?

18. If they found you in a fancy French restaurant would they expect you to be the maitre d'/hostess/busboy/waiter/chef/owner/bartender/ customer?

19. Married with children/single on the prowl?

20. Workaholic/lazy?

**Note one:** From the above exercise, cull three to six characters you'd be cast as. Work on these characters until you can do them in your sleep. (Don't wait until you have an audition.) Know how each of your characters dresses, moves, thinks, speaks, and relates to the world.

**Note two:** Just because you're going to create characters based on your appearance doesn't mean your choices have to be cliched or generic. The more creative and specific you are, the more likely you are to do memorable work.

**Note three:** If you're opposed to portraying a character that perpetuates a stereotype you find offensive, don't do it. No one can force you to take on any role. (The role will still be done; just not by you.)

**Note four:** If you don't like the way you're perceived, experiment with your appearance, e.g. hair color, style, and length; clothing; diet and exercise; eye glasses and tinted contact lenses.

*Your goal should be to get "pigeonholed" so agents will know how to market you and casting people will know what roles to bring you in on. Whether you're overweight, nerdy, the boy/girl next door, a body builder, an athlete, drop dead gorgeous, sleazy, sinister, or clean cut, do everything you can to cultivate and perpetuate that image in the minds of the people who can hire you. Once you're successful and become known for playing certain types of roles, you can then deal with the issue of showing them what else you can do.*

*Create a mold before you worry about breaking out of it.*

## YOUR ACCENT

In most cases, having an accent will limit the number of roles for which you'll be seriously considered. You don't need to get rid of your accent, but you will increase your versatility and marketability if you can do other dialects as well as your own. At the very least, if you're working in the United States, you should perfect a non-regional, standard American accent.

# NUDITY

1. Don't do anything you wouldn't want to see on cable for the next twenty years (or on the internet for eternity).

2. Doing a role with nudity will usually lead to offers of more roles with nudity. The same way that if you that you play a killer, you'll be offered more roles as killers.

3. Just because you do one "nude" role doesn't mean you have to accept another one. Your job will be to convince the industry how wonderful you are to watch with all of your clothes on.

4. If the primary focus of the project is nudity, that's primarily what you'll be remembered for.

5. Nudity in a big budget movie with Mel Gibson is perceived differently by the industry than nudity in a low budget movie with Joe Schlock.

6. Research projects the producer and director have worked on in the past to determine whether their current venture is likely to be art or exploitation.

7. It's your body, it's your decision.

8. If the director tells you there's a shower scene, but they won't really show "anything," get the specifics of what "anything" means in writing, before you show up on the set. When you get to the set, put tape over everything you don't want shown (especially if the director says, "trust me"). If he pressures you to take off more than you've agreed to, call your agent or manager.

9. Before you turn down a role with nudity, fantasize how you'll feel if the movie is wildly successful and you're not in it. Then fantasize how you'll feel if the movie is a bomb and you are in it.

10. If the most important thing an agent wants to know is if you'll do nudity, rest assured those are the types of roles he'll be submitting you for.

*Doing a nude role will certainly give you exposure, but not necessarily the kind you want.*

*Whether you make the decision on your own or someone pressures you into it, it's still your decision.*

## NEPOTISM

Look at the movie ads from any newspaper or movie magazine. Fifty percent of the stars are the children or siblings of established actors, producers, writers, directors, and casting people. Jennifer Jason Leigh, Drew Barrymore, George Clooney, Helen Hunt, Angelina Jolie, Mira Sorvino, Freddy Prinze Jr., Kate Hudson, Jamie Lee Curtis, Christian Slater, Charlie Sheen, Jeff Bridges, Bridget Fonda, Ben Stiller, Michael Douglas, Nicholas Cage, Julia Roberts, and Joaquin Phoenix are just a few of the stars who've gotten in the door (at least in part) because of who they were related to. You'd be right to complain, if it weren't for the other fifty percent of actors in those movie ads who didn't have any connections, but made it anyway. Jack Nicholson, Harrison Ford, Michelle Pfeiffer, Jim Carrey, Eddie Murphy, Denzel Washington, Clint Eastwood, Judi Dench, Sandra Bullock, Calista Flockhart, Mel Gibson, Tom Hanks, Robert DeNiro, Al Pacino, Cameron Diaz, Halle Berry, Sarah Jessica Parker, Russell Crowe, Edward Norton, Reese Witherspoon, and Billy Bob Thornton are just a few of the actors who have made it without being related to anyone in the business.

## DEMO REELS

It isn't unusual for actors to wait several months or even years to receive copies of the low budget, independent, or student films they've appeared in. If you are being paid in footage rather than cash, have the filmmakers sign a piece of paper which states, "In lieu of financial remuneration, you will hand me a copy of all of the footage in which I appear, within 60 days from today's date." If they don't sign the paper, don't do the project.

If you haven't been able to acquire the footage that show-cases you the way you want to be seen, think of a dream role, and produce it yourself. The project needn't be feature length. A five to ten minute short is long enough to accomplish your goal.

*With all the new technology, the cost of shooting your own projects is way too cheap for you to make excuses for not having film on yourself.*

## TO SHOW OR NOT TO SHOW

If agents, casting people, directors, or producers want to see film on you and your reel isn't wonderful, don't show it. (Even if they say they just want to see how you look on-camera and don't care about the quality of your work, they don't mean it.) If your work is great, but the sound and picture quality are poor, think twice before showing it. It's likely they're going to compare your tape to big budget projects from TV and film.

If you're not sure how good your reel is, show it to your act-ing coach and your fellow actors. If the feedback is "o.k." or "not bad," tell the industry people that your acting coach says your work has gotten so fantastic that your tape no longer does you justice; that you'd rather do a scene or monologue for them.

*A good rule of thumb is to assume industry people either have no imagination or are in too much of a rush to use it. Whatever you show them is exactly what they'll think you're capable of.*

*The quality of the footage is as important as the quality of your performance. The lighting, sound, and photography must be at a professional level for the work to sell you to an agent and for an agent to sell you to the industry*

## EVERYONE ELSE HAS A WEBSITE, WHY NOT YOU?

Create your own website. Include your headshot, resume, biography, and additional photos. That way when you're networking with industry people, you can give them your business card with your website address so they can learn more about you. In addition, always ask for their e-mail addresses. It's an inexpensive and efficient method to update them on your progress and to stay on top of what they're doing.

# YOU NEVER KNOW

## HAVING A "PLAN B"

For some people, having a secure day job makes them complacent, thus limiting their drive to pursue acting work. For others, having a secure day job takes the pressure off and they do better work on their auditions because they're not worried about paying the rent. For some people, having a day job they hate, motivates them to do everything they can to get acting work. For others, working a job they hate is so debilitating that they don't feel good about themselves and therefore their confidence level is low when they're auditioning. You must figure out whether you do your best work when you feel secure or when you can't stand where you are. Only then can you create the lifestyle that supports you in achieving your goals.

***You must create the lifestyle that motivates you, not everyone else.***

## RESPECT

It isn't unusual to see an actor speak in a condescending or rude manner to a secretary, assistant director, or production person. It is unusual to see the same actor behaving this way over and over because it's unlikely he'll continue to work. Remember, the secretary or assistant you are rude to today might be the casting director or producer tomorrow. But even if they're not, they do speak to the people in charge and word of obnoxious behavior spreads quickly.

*Most successful people go out of their way to treat everyone with respect.*

## GETTING FIRED

Jerry Seinfeld was fired after shooting just four episodes of "Benson." Eric McCormick of "Will and Grace" was fired from a Jenny McCarthy pilot. Ray Romano of "Everybody Loves Raymond" was fired from the pilot of "Newsradio." Hilary Swank was fired from "Bevery Hills 90210" three weeks before she was cast in "Boys Don't Cry" for which she won the Academy Award. Katherine Hepburn was fired from her first two Broadway shows. Robert DeNiro was fired from a Neil Simon film. Burt Reynolds, Clint Eastwood, and Harrison Ford were all released by Universal Pictures. Did it stop them from pursuing their dreams? Obviously not. Would it stop you?

*Is getting fired evidence that you should do something else? Or is it an opportunity to learn from your set-backs and fight on?*

*The issue is not getting fired; it's what choices you make as a result.*

## UNION DUES AND DON'TS

*"I can't get a job without first being in the union and I can't get in the union unless I first get a job."*

The truth is every single member of every single union began his or her career without union membership. They all found a way to get in. There's no reason to assume you won't.

### GETTING INTO SAG AND AFTRA:

The Screen Actor's Guild (SAG) represents actors for union productions shot on film. If you get three SAG vouchers through TV, feature, or commercial extra work you are eligible to join SAG. You can sign up with a casting service that specializes in casting extras for union productions. When you get hired as an extra, always make friends with the production person responsible for handing out the SAG vouchers. SAG signatory films are required to divide the extra work between union and non-union hires.

You can be cast in a SAG principle or speaking role (that includes commercials), without already being a member of the union. If someone really likes your work or your appearance fits what they're looking for, they can petition SAG to let you in.

Membership in SAG lets agents and casting people know that someone else already took a chance on you so they won't have to be the first. But it's not a bad idea to gain some experience and build up your credits by doing non-union projects before you worry about getting into SAG.

AFTRA (American Federation of TV and Radio Artists) is the sister union of SAG. They handle videotaped TV shows like soap operas. If you get a principle or speaking role in AFTRA (five lines and under on a Soap opera would qualify), you are eligible to join SAG after you are a member of AFTRA for one year.

AFTRA is an open union, which means there are no requirements for membership other having the money to join (over a thousand dollars). Most casting people and agents won't be overly impressed if you pay your way into AFTRA without landing a gig first.

If you get cast in a stage production under the auspices of AEA (Actor's Equity Association), you are eligible to join SAG after you are a member of AEA for one year.

**Note:** SAG and AFTRA exist to protect their members. They are not employment agencies, seeking or guaranteeing work for their members. However, you do have the opportunity to network with the industry through union sponsored seminars and workshops, as well as having access to audition hotlines and on-site casting notices.

**Note:** Qualifications for SAG and AFTRA membership subject to change. Contact SAG and AFTRA for latest requirements.

## GARBAGE IN; GARBAGE OUT

Every time you smoke, drink, do drugs, eat junk food, miss a day of exercise, fail to get enough rest, overeat or starve yourself, you're abusing the only vessel you've been given to express your art. Every time you indulge to excess, you fall a step behind.

Put down this book, go find a mirror and take a good hard look. Make a decision one way or the other and stick with it. But quit fooling yourself. In case you haven't noticed, there is no premium on prematurely aging, out of shape actors.

*Being an actor is like preparing to fight a fifteen round world championship bout. If you're not ready when the bell rings, you're gonna get knocked on your ass.*

*Filling your body with junk is like spray painting obscenities on the Mona Lisa and then expecting people to pay money to see it.*

## SORRY, WE'RE CLOSED

Imagine having your own business but only showing up for work when you felt like it. Your competition would kick your ass and you'd go broke very quickly. Guess what? If you're an actor you do have your own business. It consists of honing your craft, networking, showcasing, and self-promotion. And it can't just be a sometimes thing. You must be consistent and persistent. You must run your acting career like a business that's open 24/7 or you might as well put up the "going out of business" sign.

*Your business is to (a) make your work so excellent that you can't be ignored and (b) let everyone in the industry know that you're out there.*

*You must be consistent, persistent, and insistent. Do whatever it takes to overcome the resistant.*

## WEARING MORE THAN ONE HAT

Where would Sylvester Stallone be if he hadn't created "Rocky?" What about Chazz Palminteri's "A Bronx Tale?" Whoopee Goldberg's one woman show? Billy Bob Thorton's "Sling Blade?" Camryn Manheim's show "Wake Up, I'm Fat?" Nia Vardalos' "My Big Fat Greek Wedding?" Their enormous success is based on creating vehicles for themselves when no one else would.

You can no longer afford to say, *"I only want to act."* Whether it's writing a one person show (or getting a writer friend to do that for you), or acquiring the rights to a play, or producing a short film, or forming an improvisation group, part of your job as an artist must be to generate your own projects.

You can spend your time complaining about how unfair the business is (sexism, racism, nepotism and ageism), but if you're not excited enough to invest in a project that showcases your talent, what makes you think someone else will be? Give yourself a reason to get up in the morning. Don't be a pawn. Be a creator.

*Do not assume that people on the other side of the desk (producers, directors, casting people, agents) know any more about finding or generating good material than you do.*

## BLOWING YOUR OWN HORN

It's not enough to just let the work speak for itself. Part of your job as an actor is to let everyone know when you're working. Every time you do a speaking part on a TV show or in a film, bring a camera along (an inexpensive disposable one is sufficient) and have someone snap a photo of you. As soon as possible, get the picture copied three hundred times. (Ask for a bulk discount rate.) Send a copy to every casting director in town with a personal note on the back letting them know what you're working on. (A personal photo is more likely to get noticed than a standard postcard headshot.) If you're looking for representation, send it to every agent in town as well. Your self-promotion doesn't end there. When the project is released to theaters or it's about to air on TV, send out another postcard, reminding everyone to catch your work.

*Coke and Pepsi distinguish themselves through repetitive advertising. Can you afford to do any less?*

## HIRING SOMEONE ELSE TO BLOW YOUR HORN

Anytime you land a role with the potential for recognition, you can increase your opportunities by hiring a publicist to help to put your name and face out there. You want the world to know what you're doing so you can do more of it.

**Note:** Hiring a good publicist is expensive. To make sure you're getting your money's worth, always ask the specific steps they're going to take on your behalf, before you agree to representation.

# SECTION THREE: ACTING TECHNIQUE

*"I just couldn't wait to work with people who wanted to play as deeply as I did. Because I really believe it's a game, but I believe that what makes someone stand out is they commit themselves deeper and fuller than maybe other actors do."*
### -Ray Liotta


*"I'll tell you the same advice I always give to everyone: If you want to be an actor, act. Act as many hours of the day as you can. Act, even if you have to pay for the privilege. The more you act, the better you get. The better you get, the more success you accrue."*
### -Richard Dreyfuss

# PUSHING THE ENVELOPE

## GET OFF YOUR LAZY BUTT

If you were a writer, painter, dancer, musician, or pro athlete you would practice your craft every day. In contrast, most actors only put out maximum effort when they have an audition or they get cast in a role. Guess what? It isn't enough. *"But I'm already in class. What else can I do?"* Good question!!

1. Read at least one play or screenplay every week. Pick out a scene and break it down beat by beat.
2. Learn a new monologue.
3. Write your own monologue.
4. Do sensory work.
5. Create a weekly cold reading group with your fellow actors.
6. Join or start a theater company. If that doesn't keep you busy, join a second and a third.
7. Pick up two copies of any scene book. Sit down opposite a friend, read each scene silently and then out loud several times. Improvise the scene. Then switch roles. Don't worry about the sex or ages of the characters.
8. Go to the mall, beach, or book store and find someone who catches your eye. Observe the way they move and how they dress. Imagine what they do for a living, their history, their thoughts and their secrets. Write down your observations and create a new character.
9. If you wait tables, use the time to stimulate your imagination. Fantasize you are waiting on a Mafia boss or that you're really a king or queen hiding from your enemies. If you don't wait tables,

you're not off the hook. You can do the same creative work with any job.

10. Take singing lessons.

11. Join a dance class.

12. Listen to foreign dialect tapes when you're stuck in traffic or waiting for the bus.

13. Take a yoga class to enhance your breathing, posture, and relaxation.

14. Buy or borrow a video or digital camera and tape yourself doing commercial copy or a monologue.

15. Go to the zoo and create a character inspired by a giraffe, monkey or snake (or a combination of all three).

16. Go to the museum and create a new character inspired by a painting, sculpture, or photograph.

17. Watch a great film on video, but don't do it passively. Pick out a specific scene and watch it over and over until you can dissect the beats and the choices the actors made. What would you have done differently?

18. Re-do number 17 with a terrible movie.

19. Have intense cell phone conversations when there's no one on the other line and you have to imagine what your partner is saying.

20. Purchase Viola Spolin's Book of Improvisational Games. Invite some actors over and have an "improvisation" party.

21. Watch a video with the sound turned off to see how much the characters communicate without benefit of dialogue.

## THE COMFORT ZONE

Some actors play it safe by only working on the type of roles they have successfully done in the past. They stay within their comfort zone by only doing what they already know they can do well. It's a mistake to avoid tackling a role just because you haven't played that type of part before. Work on parts that stretch you. You'll add dimension to what you already do well and you might even surprise yourself as to what you're capable of.

Glenn Close has said one of her criteria for choosing a role is if she's not sure she can do it. Nicholas Cage received a great deal of negative feedback for his character work in "Vampires Kiss" and "Peggy Sue Got Married." That risk taking work led to his Academy Award winning performance in "Leaving Las Vegas." Sean Penn never does the same type of character twice and he is considered to be one of the best actors in the world.

*Actors become stars because they challenge themselves. They don't become stars and then challenge themselves.*

## TYING THE KNOT

The best film actors merge their own traits with those of the characters they are portraying. In "As Good As It Gets," Jack Nicholson plays a mean spirited, obsessive-compulsive writer. Jack Nicholson's sense of humor and intelligence are still evident, but they've been altered by what his character wants; how he goes after it; his obstacles; and his given circumstances. The way he thinks, moves, and communicates have been changed, but not beyond recognition. In "The Bridges of Madison County," Meryl Streep's vocal quality, accent, and physicality have been transformed, yet her essence still flows through the character. For every part you work on, ask yourself what are the essential qualities you have in common with the character and what are those that differ? The differences are the ones you'll need to focus on.

Draw a line down the middle of a sheet of paper. On the left side of the paper, make a list of the similarities between yourself and the character you are playing. On the right side, make a list of the differences. The right side is where the bulk of your work will be. If you personalize those qualities that are not naturally predominant in your personality through imagining, physicalizing, choosing strong objectives, research and observation, the character will come to life, but you won't disappear. You'll co-exist within the same physical and emotional instrument. In effect, you will have created a marriage of yourself and the character.

*The best actors create a marriage of themselves and the character. They know what qualities they inherently bring to any part they play and they allow those qualities to flow through the choices they make for their characters.*

# GETTING INSIDE A CHARACTER THAT'S NOTHING LIKE YOU

Sometimes when we read audition material, we envision the role as requiring someone very different from how we perceive ourselves. For example, perhaps you're dark, shy, and petite, but you imagine the character as a tall, voluptuous, flamboyant blonde. Rather then erasing this image from your mind, the following exercise will show you how to incorporate it into your character.

Close your eyes, take some deep breaths, and imagine you're going down a very long escalator. As you descend, tell yourself that you're going deeper and deeper and deeper into a peaceful and pleasant state of relaxation. As you come off the escalator, find yourself standing in front of a full length mirror. As you gaze into the mirror, imagine that it isn't you that you're looking at, but the character you envision as being perfect for the role. Observe that the character is dressed exactly as you'd imagined she would be; her posture, facial expressions, skin tone, hair, and eye color are ideal for the part. Hear her greet you by name and give you permission to ask her anything you want to know about her past and current circumstances. Pepper her with questions about her family, education, relationships, hobbies, taste in music and clothing, philosophy of life, religious and political beliefs, secrets, and sexuality. Ask her about her character's goals, needs, and obstacles. As she tells you about her life, slowly raise your hand and move it toward the mirror. See the character lift her hand toward you in the same manner. Feel the heat from her hand connecting the two of you. Next, see the character step out of the mirror and move toward you. Feel her gently embrace you and pull you inside of her. There is no longer a separation between you and the character. You're inside her skin. Begin to move, speak, think, and do whatever the character's impulses would lead you to do. Pick up the audition material and begin to read. Effortlessly, the character's words and world will become your own.

When you're finished working on the role, close your eyes, thank the character for her help, and tell her it's time for her to return to the mirror. See her leave your body. As you ride back up the escalator, shake out your body, and remind yourself that none of the things that happened to the character really happened to you. Your thoughts, feelings, desires, and needs belong to you and to no one else. Tell yourself that you can bring the character back to life any time you want by repeating the above process.

## DO I REALLY NEED TO KNOW WHAT COLOR SOCKS MY CHARACTER WEARS?

Actors are fond of writing elaborate character biographies, but if the history they create doesn't leap off the page and impact the character's current life then the writing will have been a waste of time. It's not the facts of your character's history, but how those facts impact who your character is now that are important.

In the film "Affliction," Nick Nolte plays an alcoholic in great emotional turmoil. When we see his father, played by James Coburn, we learn how the emotional chaos of Nick Nolte's character's formative years causes him to act out and destroy those around him. What if the film never mentioned his past through flashback and interaction with his father? Nolte would still have needed to create that biography in order to bring himself into the present. The character's past must create a path to the present or else it serves no purpose.

In another Nick Nolte film, "New York Stories," Nolte plays a painter who creates through the turmoil of unrequited love. In this film, they do not show the character's childhood through flashback and interaction with his parents, but the actor still needs to live and fantasize and research the past until it takes over his body, his movements, his thought processes, and his view of the world. Even though it isn't in the script, the past impacts the present in a very real and fervent way.

In "Sophie's Choice," Meryl Streep plays a survivor of the Nazi holocaust who is forced to sacrifice one of her children to save the other. This horrible event is shown in flashback, but even without this scene's inclusion, Meryl Streep would have needed to recreate this event as part of her preparation in order to justify the "choices" Sophie makes during the rest of the film.

In order to act in the present you must create a past that springs to life. You must fantasize and imagine every battle scar, every victory and every defeat until you can feel them take over your body, your soul, and your psyche. The biography you create must inspire you to take action in the present, otherwise it's a waste of time and paper.

Note: See CHARACTER CHECKLIST at the end of this section.

*Don't just write a character biography. Create the "flashbacks" of your character's life.*

*The biography you create must inspire you to take action in the present, otherwise it's a waste of time and paper.*

### THE BEST ACTING BOOK YOU'VE NEVER READ

Let's say you're playing a character who thinks "everyone is out to get me." If you look through a book called Diagnostic Criteria from DSM (found in the psychology section of any major book chain), you'll find a detailed list of symptoms for a paranoid personality disorder. If you're playing a violent character who's always getting arrested, read the criteria for an anti-social personality disorder. A character who thinks the world revolves around him? Look up narcissistic personality disorder. Playing a character who's depressed, or anxious, or addicted to drugs, or obsessive-compulsive, or alcoholic, or sadistic, or masochistic, or suffers from panic attacks? Diagnostic Criteria from DSM will give you detailed information for almost every dysfunctional mental state a human being can experience. And since many of the characters you're going to play are dysfunctional in some way, this book is an invaluable resource in the creation of a character.

## WHOSE YOUR DADDY?

The other characters should always be more to you than their generic labels. The character playing your dad is not just your dad. He's that *"no-good cheating bastard."* That character isn't just your math teacher; she's *"the ball-buster with the B.O."* Your boss is the *"dragon breathed slave driver."* Your girlfriend is your *"angel of mercy."* Your boyfriend is your *"lazy leach with the roving eye."*

Generic designations are not specific enough to stimulate your imagination. Your label for the other characters must include your opinion of them. This will affect how you view them and how the audience views you.

**Note one:** Examine what each of the other characters is fighting for, so you can see how your objectives mesh and conflict with theirs.

**Note two:** Time permitting, read the entire script as if you had been cast as each of the other characters. This will enhance your understanding of your own character, thereby adding emotional depth to your performance.

# HITTING THE HIGH NOTES

## "YOUR MOMENT BEFORE" IS MORE THAN WHERE YOU JUST CAME FROM

Just knowing where you came from before the scene starts isn't sufficient. If "your moment before" doesn't impact you emotionally it will have limited value. Add details that resonate with you on a gut level so you can begin the scene already immersed in the character's life. For example, if the script indicates that your character has just arrived home from work, fantasize about what might have happened on the job and/or on the way home that can put you in the emotional state necessary to begin the scene. If you need to enter in an agitated state, perhaps you were chewed out by your boss in front of your co-workers and then got stuck in rush hour traffic in the sweltering heat without any air conditioning. The bottom line is, it's highly unlikely you'll ever begin a scene from a neutral emotional state.

## WHAT'S DRIVING YOUR CHARACTER?

Your super-objective or overall goal is what your character is fighting for. It should pervade every moment of every scene. Remember Mel Gibson's work in "Braveheart?" His super-objective was to do everything within his power to gain his freedom: from wooing his mate; to keeping her memory alive; to gathering an army; to fighting the enemy; to mustering the strength to cry "freedom" as he was being tortured. Every action he took was a step towards achieving his ultimate goal.

1. Your super-objective must turn you on and inspire you to action. It must be something you ache to achieve. It can't just be an intellectual choice that you make and then forget about.
2. Your super-objective must serve the script. It can't be arbitrarily selected.
3. If you don't know your super-objective, ask yourself what is the one thing your character can't live without.

*If you're not sure of your super-objective, you'll find the answer at the end of the script. Your character will have gotten his hands on it or he will have died trying to get it or he will have learned to somehow live without it (which doesn't mean he shouldn't have gone after it in the first place).*

## PLAYING ALL THE NOTES

Actors often express one level of emotion for an entire scene. Even if that emotion is genuine, the audience will soon become bored by its repetition. The solution is to select more actions (sub-objectives) to achieve your overall goal. For example, if your overall goal is to punish your enemy, your actions might include: *to laugh at, to manipulate, to denigrate, to embarrass, to scold, to patronize, to harass, to torment, to intimidate, to conquer, to deflate, to bait, to bluff, to squash, to ignore, to freeze out,* and *to trample.* These actions are specific ways to punish your enemy that will inspire variety in your emotional expression. Remember, the more sub-objectives you use, the more notes you'll be playing, and the more dynamic your performance.

**Note:** See ACTIONS TO FULFILL YOUR OVERALL OBJECTIVE at the end of this section.

*Playing only one level of emotion is like listening to an orchestra perform only one note. No matter how well they play that note, the music will soon be drowned out by a crescendo of snoring.*

## THE MORE ROADBLOCKS, THE BETTER

In real life, we do our best to get along with other people (except when we're driving). We attempt to eliminate the obstacles that keep us from getting what we want. The opposite should hold true when we're acting. If everything is going smoothly, we're doing something wrong.

Think of it this way. In real life we want our lawns to be neatly cut and beautiful to look at. On our "dramatic lawns" the more weeds, bugs, gopher holes, crab grass, tire tracts, and snakes we have to deal with the better.

Your job as an actor is to discover as many obstacles as your given circumstances will allow. Your obstacles can be physical, emotional, spiritual, ethical, psychological, spatial, philosophical, religious, or financial. They can be internal or spring from your environment. They can be subtle or overwhelming, but if they aren't there, the audience won't be either.

*Nobody sits in a movie theater cheering, "Wow! Everyone is getting along so well and achieving their goals easily and successfully! I can't wait to see this movie again!"*

# GOING DEEPER INTO THE WORDS

Actors often ignore the magic of the words they've been given to say (unless they're doing Shakespeare). They neglect to use two very important tools that could easily assist them in adding depth and specificity to their choices; the thesaurus and the dictionary. (You may remember these two props from high school.)

Let's say the character you are portraying is described as being lonely. You can stimulate your imagination by consulting your thesaurus where you'll find the following synonyms:*forlorn, forsaken, friendless, lonesome, rejected, bleak, isolated, remote.* If you close your eyes and slowly repeat each of these words as you think about your character's given circumstances, you'll be surprised at all the wonderful images and feelings these words can evoke. Next look up lonely in your dictionary. Lonely is defined as *"dejected by the awareness of being alone," "deserted,"* and *"solitary."* Examples include *"a lonely existence," "empty of people," "the loneliest night of the week," "a lonely crossroad."* Again close your eyes and slowly repeat these definitions and examples. Allow them to permeate your being. They will be of great assistance in adding depth to the characters you are portraying.

**Note:** As part of your preparation, choose five adjectives to describe any character that you're working on. Then, using your thesaurus and dictionary, do the above exercise

## OVERCOMING BAD WRITING

*"If only the writing were better." "How can anyone play this crap?" "I'm embarrassed to say these words out loud."*

Blaming the writing is a wonderful excuse, but it won't get you the job. Your secret weapon to overcoming bad writing is subtext. Subtext goes beyond a simple paraphrasing of the author's words. Subtext includes what you really believe, what you really mean, what you really think, what you really want, what you're afraid of, what you hope for, and what you're bursting to exclaim. Your subtext must pervade every line of dialogue (for good writing as well as bad).

**EXERCISE: LINE/SUBTEXT/LINE:** Write down your subtext for each line of dialogue. Then say your subtext out loud, interspersing your words with the author's. Do this several times for each line of dialogue. Then when it comes time to actually do the scene, remnants of the subtext will flow through the author's words to create a more layered performance.

**Example:**
**Dialogue:** "Take your feet off the table."
**Subtext:** You don't respect me.
**Dialogue:** "Take your feet off the table."
**Subtext:** When we first met, you were so wonderful. You would take off your hat and even kiss my hand. You were so romantic and now look at you with that beer in your hand slobbering all over the couch, belching every five seconds."
**Dialogue:** "Take your feet off the table."
**Subtext:** I should have listened when my mother warned me about

you. I could have married Harry. He was a successful accountant. He knew how to respect women. So he wasn't good in bed. Sex isn't everything. You proved that.

**Dialogue:** "Take your feet off the table."

**Subtext:** I resent the fact that you made me quit my job when we got married. I could have had a career, my own money, my own life. Instead I'm trapped here with you.

**Dialogue:** Take your feet off the table.

**Subtext:** My dad used to sit with his feet up like he was "King Tut" and the rest of us were his slaves. Well, I won't put up with it anymore.

**Dialogue:** "Take your feet off the table."

**Subtext:** I'm afraid to tell you what's really bothering me so I'll focus on the superficial bullshit.

The following example shows how subtext can change the entire meaning of a scene:

**Dialogue:** "What's for dinner?"

**Subtext:** I don't need food when I'm with you. You're so beautiful I can't even eat. You take my breath away.

**Dialogue:** "Pass the mustard."

**Subtext:** "I want to spread it all over your body and lick it off.

(Same dialogue. Different given circumstances)

**Dialogue:** "What's for dinner?"

**Subtext:** I hope we don't have that same lousy meat loaf just because it's the only thing you can cook without burning down the house.

**Dialogue:** "Pass the mustard."

**Subtext:** I need something to mask the taste of this swill you're trying to kill me with.

**104**

**Note one:** Your subtext must be inspired by the tone, content, and style of the project you are working on. You can't arbitrarily attach a subtext that doesn't support the story you are helping to tell.

**Note two:** In addition to overcoming bad writing, the "Line/ Subtext/Line" method is an excellent tool for memorization.

*It takes a great actor to bring mediocre writing to life. That's why they thought of you for the role in the first place.*

*Creating a character is like building a house. The author's words are the blueprint. Your subtext is the brick and mortar.*

## CHARACTERS DON'T ALWAYS SAY WHAT THEY MEAN

Characters always mean more than they're saying. Sometimes they even mean the complete opposite of what they're saying. If a character asks what time it is, she may be flirting or getting ready to steal someone's watch. She doesn't really care what the correct time is unless a bomb she planted didn't explode when it should have, she needs an alibi, or she's late for her own wedding or funeral. Nothing is communicated just for informational purposes. That's why your subtext (see OVERCOMING BAD WRITING in this section) is so important.

**Sample dialogue:**
**Bill:** Where were you last night? (*Just because Bill asks Mary where she was last night doesn't mean Bill doesn't already know or at least suspect where Mary really was. Maybe he even followed her.*)
**Mary:** I was out bowling with my girlfriends.
(*Just because Mary says she was out bowling last night doesn't mean she wasn't doing something more mysterious or exciting.*)
**Bill:** I was just wondering.
(*Bill is just wondering how stupid Mary thinks he is.*)
**Mary:** Whatever.
(*Mary is wondering what she ever found remotely appealing about Bill in the first place.*)

**Note:** The deeper meaning you attach to each line of dialogue is not arbitrarily selected, just to be interesting or clever. It must fulfill the author's intention, serve the material, and advance the plot. Your job is not to rewrite the screenplay, but to add depth to the story already being told.

## WORDS VS. BEHAVIOR

Actors often fail to explore possible dichotomies between words and actions. Just because the line says *"I love you"* doesn't mean you can't be stuffing your face with french fries or looking at yourself admiringly in the mirror when you say it. Just because the line says *"I hate you"* doesn't mean you can't be slow dancing with the object of your scorn when you say it. Just because the line says *"You're dead meat,"* doesn't mean you can't be engrossed in a crossword puzzle or gently pinching the other character's cheek when you say it.

Take a look at the scene in "Remains of the Day," where Emma Thompson's character enters Anthony Hopkins' room and attempts to pry a book out of his hands. Emma Thompson's non-verbal behavior goes way beyond an inquiry into Anthony Hopkins' reading preferences to reveal her deep seated passion and his emotional paralysis.

**Note:** Your behavioral choices must always serve the material. They cannot be arbitrarily selected just to be interesting or clever.

## YOUR PIECE OF THE PUZZLE

*"As long as I understand my own role, why should I have to read the whole thing?" "My part is so small it doesn't even impact the rest of the story."*

First of all, if your role were so unimportant it wouldn't have been included in the first place. Secondly, how can you possibly understand the tone, style, and genre if you haven't read the entire script?

Imagine someone was making a giant patch quilt and you'd been hired to design one of the squares. Wouldn't you want to know what fabrics, designs, and colors were being used in the rest of the quilt before you sewed your square? Of course you would, because no matter how interesting your patch, if it didn't fit in with the rest of the quilt it would stand out like an eye sore. It's the same thing with filmmaking. The script is the material you've been given to weave your performance. Use it and your part will fit seamlessly. Ignore it and everything begins to unravel.

# THE PLEASURE IN THE PAIN

## KEEPING YOUR EMOTIONAL PREPARATION FRESH

One of the common mistakes actors make is to worry that using a memory over and over for emotional preparation will cause it to "dry up." This won't happen if you (a) get more specific each time you conjure up a past event and (b) add more details.

For example, let's say you're using the loss of your pet dog to spark your emotional preparation. When you began using this memory it would bring tears to your eyes, but now through repetition you're finding its power to be diluted. Rather than abandoning this memory, get more specific. Don't just focus on the actual demise of your pet. Recall details from the entire relationship, e.g. the day you went to the pound with your parents to pick out your puppy; the hours you two spent playing frisbee in the park; the time you finally got your dog to sit on command; the dog jumping in your arms and licking your face when you came home from school; the growling noise it made when the mailman came; the way you rubbed its belly when the two of you watched TV together.

Now add new details to the events leading up to the dog's demise;  the sound, feel, and sight of the dog panting or crying as you carried it in your arms to the vet's office; the tone of the vet's voice and the expression on her face when she told you it would be best if the dog were put down; the facial, vocal, and physical reactions of your family members as you told them what you'd had to do.

By adding sensory details and discovering forgotten aspects of your recollections, you'll add emotional depth to your performance and you'll no longer have to worry about your memories "drying up."

## LETTING GO OF YOUR EMOTIONAL PREPARATION

Actors often worry that they'll drop their emotional preparation and fall out of the scene. They're forgetting that the purpose
of an emotional preparation is to get them involved in the character's life. It isn't to carry them through the entire scene.

Imagine you were getting ready to go out on a date with
someone you really liked. While you were dressing you might be
thinking about all the things that attracted you to this person in the
first place, i.e. their appearance, their sense of humor, their passion,
the sound of their voice, their smile. You might be fantasizing about
what it would be like if the two of you got married; how many children you'd have, where you'd live, etc. But when the doorbell
finally rang and your date had arrived you wouldn't be thinking,
*"I'm excited now but what if half way through the date I can't hold
onto the loving feelings I built up before they got here?"* If this person brought you flowers, made you laugh, kissed you, told you how
attractive you looked, or danced with you, your loving feelings
would most likely continue. If they flirted with someone else, made
fun of your hair, farted non-stop, or talked incessantly on their cell
phone, your feelings would probably change.

Guess what? It's the same thing when you're acting. When
the door bell rings (the director calls action), your emotional preparation must get you to the front door but once you open it, your feelings are going to change as a result of what you get from and give
to your partner.

**Note:** Actors are often told to do their homework and then to
"throw it all away." A reasonable question might be, if you're just
going to throw away your homework, why did you need to do it in
the first place? The phrase, "throwing away your homework" really means, if you've done a good solid preparation, you can trust that
the choices you've made are in your body and you don't need to

think about them. It doesn't mean you didn't need to make those choices in the first place.

## FORCING THE EMOTION

Sometimes, actors appear to be squeezing out emotion as if they were constipated. They're pressuring themselves to manufacture the emotion they think they're supposed to be feeling. They're forgetting that emotion is a by-product of objectives being thwarted by obstacles. The emotion itself is never the intention.

If you find yourself pushing the emotion, it's because you haven't made strong enough choices. Raise the stakes by making your goals more evocative, specific, and immediate. Create stronger obstacles, personalize your character's given circumstances, and rework your moment before. And last but not least, do some relaxation exercises, because if you're tense the emotion won't have any way to find release from your body (even if it's there).

## CRYING ON CUE

Think of an event from your life where you experienced some sadness or suffered a loss. Were you saying to yourself, *"Gee, I hope I can cry when I'm supposed to,"* or *"Thank God I'm really crying!"* Of course not! The emotion resulted from your immersion in your real life circumstances. It should be the same thing when you're acting. If you're really involved in the life of your character, the emotion will take care of itself.

*"But what do I do if I'm immersed in the character's given circumstances, have a strong moment before, objectives I ache to*

*achieve, obstacles driving me up the wall and I still can't cry?"*
Excellent question! The following are some steps to help you
explore other ways to release your character's pent up emotion.

**1. REVERSE PSYCHOLOGY:** For some actors it's about telling
yourself in character not to cry. *"Even if she leaves me, I'm not
going to cry." "I refuse to let them see me cry." "No matter what
they do to me, I won't break down."* Tears will often result because
you are removing the pressure and obligation to cry.

**2. THE OUTSIDE IN:** Place your body in the position you were
in when you have cried in real life and begin to move, breath, and
let out the sounds you would make if you were really crying. It may
seem awkward and artificial at first, but if you practice this technique on a daily basis, your body's muscle memory will eventually
allow this to become real.

**Note one:** Do not wait until you have an audition or you're on the
set to begin your exploration of this method.

**Note two:** If you don't cry in real life, see REVEALING EMO-
TIONS in the BREAKING FREE OF MENTAL BARRIERS section of this book.

**3. THE INSIDE OUT:** Think of a past experience that caused you
great sadness. Recreate the circumstances leading up to this event
as if it were happening right now. Use all five of your senses. Be
very specific as to what you see, hear, taste, touch, and smell. Don't
worry about the result and don't try to squeeze out the emotion. This
isn't a documentary of your life, it's a creative exploration so if
you're stuck, you can change any or all of the variables of the memory. You can change how old you were or what you were wearing,
what was being said to you or who was saying it. If your imagina-

tion isn't sparked, select another event. If you can sensorially recreate the circumstances leading up this event, you'll be surprised how easily the tears will flow.

**4. BACK DOOR MEMORY:** Let's say the scene is about the death of your character's mother. If thinking about the mother's last moments doesn't move you, focus on the prior circumstances. Examples: imagine the time your character's mother sang you a lullaby and rocked you to sleep when you were a toddler; the time you walked hand in hand to your first day of kindergarten; the day she taught you to ride a bicycle; how she cried when you graduated from high school. Why should you be moved by the death of another character if you haven't created the life that would allow you to miss them in the first place?

**5. POWER PHRASE:** Select a phrase that fits the character you are playing and repeat it silently several times before you begin the scene. Pick something that really moves you. e.g. *"Nobody loves me"* or *"Please don't leave me"* or *"Why can't I ever do anything right?"*

**6. MUSIC:** Select a piece of music that evokes a strong memory. Perhaps it's the music that was playing when you met the love of your life or the music you blasted to drown out your parents' fighting. It may not have made you cry at the time, but it might put you in the necessary state, if used in combination with the character's given circumstances. Bring a walkman with you and play this music while you're waiting to read or perform.

**7. PLACE:** A strong sense of place may trigger the tears. Create a place from your past and/or your imagination that evokes painful or wonderful memories. Again use all five of your senses.

**8. PERSONAL OBJECTS:** Wear an item of jewelry or place something in your pocket that has a strong association for you. Then touch it or look at it before you start the scene. This personal object can be from your past or you can endow it with personal associations from your imagination.

**9. USE IT:** If you're feeling frustrated and defeated because you aren't able to cry, attribute those feelings to the character.

**10. SIGHT LIGHT:** Henry Fonda used to stare at the brightest light he could find without blinking until his eyes began to water.

**11. SOMEONE ELSE:** Quite often we're more empathetic to someone else's plight than we are to our own. If your character's given circumstances don't move you, imagine they're happening to someone else.

**Note:** It isn't unusual to see actors having eucalyptus blown through their eyes by "wardrobe" in order to evoke tears. This is perfectly acceptable, but only helpful if the tears are to come at the beginning of the scene.

*If your primary reason for crying is because "the script says you're supposed to," your focus is in the wrong place.*

*It's not about whether you cry. It's about whether the audience cries.*

*How you cry is as important as whether you cry. You don't cry the same way at a wedding as you do at a funeral or when your team loses or when you stub your toe.*

## FINDING THE PLEASURE

A mistake actors make is to fail to find pleasure in the playing, no matter how painful the character's given circumstances. Even if your character is being tortured, you must enjoy the exquisiteness of the situation; the absurdity of the game, the challenge of being trapped in a seemingly irrevocable situation that you must fight to overcome.

One of the reasons Jack Nicholson is so successful is that he finds the pleasure in everything his characters experience. This is a man who truly loves to act and that's why audiences enjoys watching him. Take a look at the scene in "A Few Good Men" where he is being cross examined on the witness stand. Even though he is caught in a lie that will ruin his life, you can almost catch him beaming. He's a soldier who loves the battle and he won't go down without a fight. Remember Robert Redford and Paul Newman in the final scene from "Butch Cassidy and the Sundance Kid?" Their characters are about to be massacred, yet they're still savoring their future heists. These actors teach us it's not enough just to play the truth. There must always be pleasure in the playing.

*The pleasure in the playing comes from choosing an objective that inspires you to action, no matter how horrible your character's given circumstances.*

*If you don't savor the trap your character is ensnared in, why would you think we as an audience would enjoy watching it?*

*No matter how painful the given circumstances, always ask yourself, "How can I make this a game?"*

# DID YOU SAY SOMETHING?

## THE SOUND OF YOUR OWN VOICE

*"Why did I say the line that way?" "My voice sounds so breathy." "Oh that sounded really good." "That sounded really phony."*

Listening to yourself is an attempt to control how you sound so you can avoid appearing foolish. The only thing it actually accomplishes is to create self-conscious, predictable acting. In contrast, inspired work manifests when your focus of attention is on what you want, not how you sound. If you immerse yourself in your character's given circumstances and put your complete attention on your partner, you won't have the time or the need to listen to yourself.

*If you're listening to yourself, you're not acting, you're critiquing.*

## WAITING FOR THE OTHER ACTOR TO SHUT UP

Actors sometimes think they're acting only when it's their turn to speak. They seem to be waiting for the other actor to shut up so they can deliver their next line. The reality is that they're not listening and if they're not listening they might as well be acting by themselves.

*Listening is the fuel that creates the need for your verbal response.*

116

## DIALECTS

1. If you're creating a character with a dialect other than your own, work on the accent until you can do it without thinking about it. Otherwise, your focus will be on listening to yourself, rather than connecting with the other characters.

2. If you don't have access to a dialect coach, your best bet is to tape record someone who comes from the same place as your character. If you don't know anyone personally, be creative, e.g. if you need a French accent, locate a restaurant that serves French food. You're likely to find an employee with that dialect. Ask if you can tape record him doing some of the dialogue from your script. (You might have to eat some French food while you're there.)

3. You have access to radio stations from all over the world through the internet. Start listening.

4. Purchase dialect tapes from your local drama book or from Amazon.com. Tapes of inhabitants of the actual locale are recommended.

5. If you have limited time to prepare, rent a film with a character who comes from the same place as the one you're playing.

*Do you think Meryl Streep would have achieved her level of success if she could only speak with the accent she grew up with?*

## USING PROPS CREATIVELY

Using props just to look busy is a common mistake actors make. If you're going to use props, they must (a) help the character fulfill her objectives in the most truthful and creative ways possible and (b) bring the character's given circumstances to life.

Let's say the circumstances of your scene are as follows: a couple has been married for four years, but they haven't made love in months and the wife suspects infidelity is the root cause. She is waiting for her husband to get home. The actor has been directed to iron and fold laundry which is a very popular activity (particularly in acting classes), despite the fact that it's not usually very interesting to watch. The actor's job is to figure out how to do this mundane activity in the most creative way possible. For example, while ironing she might stick her nose in her husband's clothes to pick up the scent of another woman's perfume; go through his pants' pockets, searching for receipts from romantic restaurants and/or Victoria's Secret; and/or examine the collar of his dress shirt, searching for microscopic red marks that could only be lipstick. Once she found the evidence (or even if she didn't), she might crumple and stomp on all of her husband's neatly stacked clothing, imagining it's him she is pulverizing, or she might take a pair of scissors and cut out the crotches from all of his Calvin Klein underwear.

Using the same props, let's change our given circumstances to the following: a rebellious teenager has stayed out all night, despite repeated warnings from her parents that she would be grounded for life. As punishment, she is being forced to iron and fold her entire family's laundry. If her goal is to pay her parents back for her "unfair" punishment, she might "accidentally on purpose" spill her coke on her mom's best blouse as she irons; fold the clothes in a way that makes them look more wrinkled than they did before she ironed; and/or burn a hole in her mom's best blouse because she "just wasn't paying attention."

Using the same props, let's change our given circumstances one more time: an unmarried couple is living together. The woman is ironing her boyfriend's shirts while he is away on a business trip. In this scenario, she suspects when he gets home he's going to propose marriage. How does this information affect the way she irons and folds? Does she glide the iron across his shirt, imagining it's his body she's caressing? Does she gently lift his shirt up to her face and breathe in the most beautiful aroma in the world? Does she place his shirt around her shoulders and dance around the room, imagining it's his arms that are wrapped around her?

Take a look at Jack Lemmon's work in the film "The Apartment." Towards the end of the film, he is making spaghetti for the woman he loves, only he doesn't have a colander so he is straining the pasta through the holes in his tennis racket as he sings to himself. He is doing what could easily be a mundane activity in a way that not only shows the joy he is feeling, but reveals a bachelor in need of someone to take care of him. We can see that it's not the activity itself, but the specificity and creativity that will determine the difference between an audience's boredom and fascination.

**Note**: Your props and activities must always serve the material and move you toward the fulfillment of your objective.

***Either pick props and activities that excite you or do ordinary activities in an extraordinary way. Don't take the easy way out. You'll be bored and so will your audience.***

## TELEPHONE ETIQUETTE

Many of us spend half of our lives yakking on the telephone. We wield our cell phones like Darth Vader brandishes his sword. Yet when it comes time to doing scenes that take place over the phone, we fail to use all of this incredible training.

1. Actors often fail to take advantage of the fact that in a telephone scene the off-camera character can't see the on-camera character's behavior. Let's say you're doing a telephone scene where you're telling your parents how hard you're studying while you're away at college and that you need more money for books. If prior circumstances indicate that you're homesick, you might be twisting the phone cord to keep from crying. If prior circumstances indicate that you're a scam artist, you might be trying to make your voice sound whiny or weepy while at the same time you're channel surfing, reading a comic, and using your school books as a footstool. In either case, you're going beyond the contents of the phone call to create behavior that will allow the audience to gain further insight into your character.

**Note:** In many cases, sitting still and responding simply and truthfully best serves the material.

2. When you're doing a telephone scene where the audience can only hear your portion of the dialogue, you must make us believe you're really speaking to someone on the other line. The best way to create this illusion is to rehearse with another actor. Have him improvise the off-camera dialogue that would fit with your responses. Do this several times until you can imagine the other person's rejoinders even when they're silent.

3. If the audience is privy to only your side of the conversation, you needn't hear every single word being said to you. The gist of the off-camera dialogue will suffice to keep the pace of the scene moving. This is parallel to doing a scene where your character is eating a meal. If you actually had to chew and swallow every single bite, a two minute scene would take an hour and a half to play.

4. Try adding uh huhs, yeahs, and hmmms, as you would in real life. The tone and pace of these utterances can go a long way toward revealing your interest or boredom in the conversation.*

*Subject to directorial approval.

5. Actors have a tendency to look down when they're doing telephone scenes because they're not sure where to focus their attention. If you're really listening, you're concentrating on comprehending and processing the words in your mind's eye. In effect, you're looking within. The camera must be able to see your eyes in order to register your thoughts, but you needn't focus on anything concrete.

## GETTING TO THE GOOD PART

When an actor is performing the climactic portions of the script, her commitment and creativity are at peak levels and her juices are flowing. In contrast, the scenes that set up the conflict sometimes receive short shrift. It often seems as if the actor is killing time waiting to get to the good parts.

Think of it this way. Imagine you were an architect commissioned to build an entire house from scratch. Your client's instructions include sparing no expense in the creation of the kitchen. So you go to work leaving no stone unturned in your construction of the most fantastic kitchen imaginable. Finally the big day arrives. The house has been completed and the client has arrived. You check the kitchen one more time. *"Wait until they see it. It's perfect!"* As you rush to greet your client you notice that you neglected to put windows in the living room and the bathroom has no toilet. Not to mention that the entire house is lopsided. The kitchen is beautiful, but the structure around it is collapsing. You've forgotten that the owner has to live in the entire house, not just the kitchen. You've neglected the cardinal rule of home building and acting: if you don't grab the buyer/audience when they come in the front door, it won't matter how fantastic the kitchen/climax is.

This problem is often reinforced in acting classes where only the climactic portions of the script are worked on. As an exercise, select the least dramatic scene you can find. Approach this material not only as if it's the best part of the entire story, but the only part you'll ever work on. This mind set will force you to make every moment as specific, distinctive, and alive as possible.

## THE OUTCOME

When we're acting, we know how everything's going to turn out. (Hopefully, we've read the script.) The upside is knowing the outcome gives us information we can use to make our character's journey as challenging as possible. The downside is the excitement of moment to moment play may be reduced or eliminated because subconsciously we may be saying to ourselves, *"Why bother fighting for what I want? I already know whether I'm going to get it or not."*

The following exercise will train your mind to let go of what you know is going to happen to the character you are playing:

Fantasize in detail about the best things that could possibly happen to your character. Then fantasize in detail about the worst things that could possibly happen. Share these possible outcomes with your scene partner and have them share their best and worse possible scenarios.* Then improvise each scene using the best and worst case scenarios each of you has come up with. Do this several times. Then right before you perform each scene, silently say to yourself three times, *"I have no idea how all this is going to turn out."* This preparation will allow you to play moment to moment, despite your knowledge of the outcome.

*If there isn't time to work with your scene partner or you would prefer to keep this part of your preparation a secret, you may choose to do this exercise with an actor who isn't involved in this particular project.

*The actor always knows how the scene is going to turn out. The character she is playing has no idea.*

## WHEN YOU'RE FINISHED WORKING

If you've taken the time to imagine yourself into a role, you must take the time to remove yourself when you're finished working on it. For example, if you're playing a character that has been damaged by a personal tragedy or trauma, you've no doubt spent a considerable amount of time personalizing the material. When you're finished with the part, shake out your body and tell yourself that the things that happened to the character didn't really happen to you; that you're safe from any and all harm. Then fantasize that you're somewhere pleasant, perhaps relaxing on the beach with a close friend with whom you can be yourself. If you don't take the time to remove yourself from a role filled with emotional turmoil, you might walk around depressed, angry, or fearful for several days and not know why. Not only will that interfere with your personal life, but it may cause your work on one role to bleed into the next.

# THE CHECKLIST

## WHAT IS A METHOD ACTOR ANYWAY?

Method acting is a technique to bring the actor to the material in a truthful, personal, and creative way. The "method" gives the actor the tools to experience what the character is going through (as opposed to indicating or faking it). The father of method acting is Russian acting teacher Constantin Stanislavski, whose three most well known American disciples were Lee Strasberg, Stella Adler, and Sanford Meisner. Much of Lee Strasberg's work centered on encouraging the actor to draw on emotional parallels from his own past to create the character (working from the inside out). Stella Adler emphasized imagination and physicality directly relating to the text to create the character (working from the outside in). Sanford Meisner focused on getting the actor's attention off himself and onto the other characters by developing listening skills to create truthful "moment to moment" behavior.

Debating which technique is best is like wondering whether a hammer, saw, or screwdriver is the most valuable tool to have around the house. Why not use all three? Use your imagination and observational skills to get inside the character. Find emotional parallels from your own life to personalize the material and get your focus of attention on the other actors by really listening. In short, draw from all methods and means to create your own box of tools. That way you'll be able to fix anything that's not working or build something new from scratch.

## YOU NEED ACTING CLASSES. YES, YOU

*"I don't need to take classes. I'm a natural."*

You may be incredibly talented, but so are Brando, DeNiro, and Meryl Streep, all of whom had years of training. Even if you're one of those actors who starred in every high school production and majored in theater in college, it is strongly suggested that you actively participate in acting classes at least once a week to hone and expand your skills and then to keep them at peak performance level. An ideal class should include cold readings, technique, and prepared scene work. If you are pursuing a career in TV and film, your classes should be on-camera to allow you to become comfortable and knowledgeable working in this medium. In addition, it is strongly suggested that you work with a professional coach every time you have an audition. Why? Because that's what your competition is doing and you need to give yourself every edge.

*"Whenever we dig down into the achievements of a creative artist, we invariably trace them to the beginning of all beginnings; labor."*
**-Galina Ulanova, Ballerina**

*Having talent is one thing. Having the technique to manifest and sustain a career is another.*

## CHARACTER CHECKLIST

(see DO I REALLY NEED TO KNOW WHAT COLOR SOCKS MY CHARACTER IS WEARING in this section)

1. What is your character's fundamental belief and philosophy about herself and the world? e.g. *"Life is a wonderful adventure"* *"Never let your guard down."* How does that belief/philosophy infuse everything your character says and does?
2. Does your character have a job? Does she love, resent, or despise her work? What would her dream job be? If she doesn't work, what does she do for money?
3. What is your character's relationship with money?
4. Is your character wealthy/middle class/poverty stricken?
5. What is her living environment like? Does she live in a trailer park/ apartment/farm/mansion?
6. Does she live alone/roommates/family?
7. Is she married/single/divorced/children?
8. What is it about her life is she most driven to change?
9. Is your character in love? If so, how long have she and her partner been together? Is it a healthy or troubled relationship?
10. Has your character ever suffered a broken heart?
11. Is your character's sexuality a source of pride/power/shame?
12. How does she behave around the opposite sex? Confident/insecure/sexually experienced/naive?
13. How does your character behave around people of the same sex? Competitive/insecure/arrogant/talkative/secretive/distrustful?
14. Is your character comfortable inside her own skin?
15. Has she ever betrayed/teased/embarrassed/worshipped someone?
16. Has she ever been betrayed/teased/embarrassed/worshipped?
17. What are the most important things your character learned

about herself and the world while growing up?

18. Did she come from a family with secrets? How do those secrets impact her current situation?

19. Was she the black sheep/hero/clown/troublemaker in her family?

20. What is your character's Achilles heel? (Fatal flaw)

21. Where is your character's power center in her body? How does that affect the way she moves? Does she glide/saunter/lumber/swagger/ strut/slink/burst into a room?

22. Is she graceful/clumsy/athletic?

23. Is her posture relaxed/rigid/slouching?

24. What part of her body is your character most vain about? Uncomfortable with?

25. Vocal qualities: Does she talk rapidly/slowly? Articulate/tongue-tied/loud/soft-spoken/lisp/stutter/accent?

26. Any physical impediments/handicaps?

27. Any mental handicaps/deficiencies?

28. What sensation is most acute for this character? Seeing/hearing/tasting/touching/smelling?

29. What geographical location is she from?

30. How old is your character? Is her age a source of comfort/shame/confidence? Does her age make her feel as if she's beginning a great adventure or running out of time?

31. How much education has your character received? What is she smart/dumb about? Is she street smart/gullible?

32. What is her personality type? Vain/friendly/outgoing/shy/gregarious/dynamic/selfish/generous/petty/lazy/jealous/cowardly/risk taker/prudish/flamboyant?

33. Does she have a sense of humor? Even about herself? What makes her laugh?

34. What does your character believe about herself that she would never tell anyone?

35. Alcohol/drug use/smoker/caffeine/sugar use/favorite foods/eating disorders?

36. Any fears or phobias?

37. How does your character dress? Stylishly/sloppily? Which parts of her body do her clothing highlight/hide?

38. What are your character's political and religious beliefs?

39. Any hobbies?

40. What type of music turns her on? What type of music drives her up a wall?

41. Does she like animals? Any pets?

42. What does this character carry in her pockets or purse?

43. What's the worst thing this character has ever done to herself?

44. What's the most wonderful thing this character has ever done for anyone? For herself?

45. What is this character's greatest regret?

46. What animalistic qualities does your character have? Piggish/wolfish/snake-like/catty/swan-like/ratty/stool pigeon? How does that affect the way she moves, speaks, thinks?

47. Are there photos or art work from books/magazines/museums/C.D. covers that can stimulate your imagination in the creation of your character?

48. Is there someone you know or have observed who has qualities you can incorporate into your character?

49. Are there book/video/internet sources you can draw on in the creation of your character?

50. What emotion is the easiest for your character to express? Most difficult?

51. What is the worst thing someone else could say about your character? The best?

52. What makes your character's blood boil? Brings her the most joy?

53. What is your character's recurring dream or nightmare?

54. After she dies, what would your character expect others to say about her? What would the epitaph on her tombstone be?

*All human beings communicate who they really are the moment they enter a room. The characters you create can afford to do no less.*

## ACTIONS TO FULFILL YOUR OVERALL OBJECTIVE

(see PLAYING ALL THE NOTES in this section)

| | | |
|---|---|---|
| to abandon | to blame | to compete |
| to accept | to blast | to compliment |
| to accuse | to bluff | to con |
| to admire | to boast | to concoct |
| to admit | to bore | to condemn |
| to admonish | to brag | to condescend |
| to affirm | to break out | to confess |
| to agonize | to break away | to conspire |
| to amuse | to bruise | to contain |
| to annihilate | to burden | to control |
| to annoy | to burn | to convince |
| to apologize | to cajole | to cool off |
| to appease | to calm down | to corrupt |
| to argue | to captivate | to cover |
| to assault | to capture | to covet |
| to assert | to castrate | to criticize |
| to assure | to celebrate | to crush |
| to attack | to challenge | to curse |
| to avoid | to charm | to damn |
| to awaken | to chase | to dare |
| to bait | to cheat | to deceive |
| to barter | to chew out | to defend |
| to beat | to choke | to defy |
| to beg | to claim | to degrade |
| to belittle | to cling | to delight |
| to berate | to coax | to demand |
| to betray | to comfort | to demonstrate |
| to blackmail | to command | to demote |

| | | |
|---|---|---|
| to denounce | to help | to nag |
| to deny | to hide | to nail |
| to destroy | to hint | to negotiate |
| to detain | to ignore | to oppose |
| to devastate | to imitate | to order |
| to elude | to impress | to overthrow |
| to embarrass | to inflame | to overwhelm |
| to enchant | to inspire | to own |
| to encourage | to instigate | to pacify |
| to enlighten | to insult | to patronize |
| to entice | to interrogate | to permit |
| to eradicate | to intimidate | to persecute |
| to face | to investigate | to persuade |
| to fight | to invite | to pester |
| to flatter | to judge | to pierce |
| to flirt | to justify | to placate |
| to find | to kiss ass | to plant |
| to forbid | to kick ass | to plead |
| to force | to lash out | to rationalize |
| to forgive | to lead | to reassure |
| to free | to lecture | to rebel |
| to frighten | to liberate | to recover |
| to gloat | to love | to refuse |
| to goad | to lunge | to reject |
| to gossip | to lure | to repel |
| to grab | to lust | to repent |
| to grieve | to menace | to repress |
| to grill | to mimic | to resist |
| to grope | to mock | to retreat |
| to ground | to mother | to reward |
| to grovel | to mourn | to ridicule |

| | | |
|---|---|---|
| to shove | to stall | to undermine |
| to slap | to startle | to unite |
| to smash | to taunt | to urge |
| to smooth | to teach | to veto |
| to snub | to tempt | to violate |
| to soothe | to terrify | to vow |
| to spin | to test | to warn |
| to spoil | to threaten | to weaken |
| to spurn | to tickle | to withhold |
| to squeeze | to trap | to woo |
| to stab | to unburden | to worship |

# SECTION FOUR: WORKING ON THE SET

*"On the stage I perform. In film I behave."*
-Brian Denehy

*Go into yourself and give from your soul.*

# ON YOUR MARK

## THE CAMERA

Actors often perceive the camera in a way that causes them to feel insecure. Some see the camera as a "bullshit meter" ready to tell the world what a fraud they are. Others feel like the bull's eye in the cross hairs of a cannon. Some actors relate to the camera as if it were an alien invader, a giant cyclops that never blinks or looks away. Regarding the camera in any of these ways will most certainly keep you from doing your best work.

The truth is the camera has no thoughts or feelings, so if you're feeling intimidated, you are projecting your own insecurities. The following adjustments will help to transform your relationship to the camera:

1. If you're going to attribute qualities to the camera, why not perceive it as a best friend or a lover; someone who wants you to succeed and loves to watch you play; someone you couldn't possibly be intimidated by? Give the camera the name of someone who meets this criteria. Then every time you're on the set, greet the camera (silently) by name, tell it how much fun the two of you are going to have, wink and give it a tiny wave or salute.

2. Imagine you were a painter and you had a clean white canvas you were about to paint on. Would you be afraid the canvas would expose you as a fraud? Laugh at you behind your back? Shoot you down? Chew you up and spit you out? Of course not! You can splash whatever colors and shapes you desire onto your canvas. The canvas itself has no opinion one way or the other. It is merely the vehicle for the expression of your creativity. It's the same thing

135

with the camera. It has no opinion of your work. It is only the canvas upon which you are choosing to paint.

3. If, while you are working, your primary focus is on the camera, your prior circumstances need to be stronger, the stakes need to be higher, and your relationships with the other characters need to be more specific.

4. Whenever you're on the set (without making a pest of yourself) observe how the cinematographer sets up each camera shot, which lenses she uses, how the camera woman handles the camera, what the focus puller does, etc. Good actors take the time to understand all the tools they are working with, not just their own instrument.

*"If you love the camera, it will love you back."*
**- Michael Caine**

*The camera has no opinion of your work. It is only the canvas upon which you are choosing to paint.*

## CLOSE-UPS

Some actors do great work during the master (wide shot covering the entire scene) and the medium shots, but feel intimidated when the camera comes in for their close-up. If this is true for you, spend more time on relaxation and personalization and create a stronger moment before. In addition, make sure to get your full attention on the other actor. Don't make the close-up about you, the actor. Think of it as another angle on the story your character is helping to tell.

## THE FRAME OF YOUR CLOSE-UP

If you don't know how tight the camera lens is going to be for your close-up, you won't know how much you can move without going out of frame. If the director of photography doesn't give you this information, don't be afraid to ask. It will demonstrate your professionalism and your knowledge of the craft of filmmaking.

## LESS IS MORE (SOMETIMES)

The mistake inexperienced film actors make is thinking "less is more" means you can just show up, stand there, mumble your lines and you're off to the Golden Globes. Guess what? You still have to make as many choices and have the same degree of specificity as you would if you were doing a play. The only difference is, instead of projecting what you're doing, feeling and saying, you're containing it. Remember, the camera can only pick up the fullness of your experience if you're actually having an experience.

*Sometimes less is more. Sometimes less is less.*

## LETTING THE CAMERA DO ITS JOB

The theater actor experiences what the character is going through and projects that experience to the audience. The film actor experiences what the character is going through, but allows the camera to project that experience to the audience. If the film actor doesn't let the camera do its job, she will appear to be doing too much and working too hard.

*The film actor thinks loudly and speaks softly.*

*In film, the audience should be more interested in what you're thinking than what you're saying.*

## EYE MOVEMENT

Film actors are taught how important the eyes are for the communication of thought and feeling. The problem occurs when the actor exaggerates her eye movement so the other actors and the audience don't miss anything. If you really experience what your character is going through, everyone will see it. If you consciously use your eyes to show the audience what's going on with you, you'll be doing way too much.

## BLINKING AND GESTURING

Constantly blinking and emphasizing everything you say with hand gestures and excessive head movement are indications of nervous tension and/or habitual behavior on the part of the actor, not the character being portrayed. (Unless the character is a nervous, self-conscious neurotic.) Watch good actors on the big screen. Their feelings and thoughts come across even when they're completely still.

If your blinking and gesturing is habitual and excessive, do not wait until you're working on the set to get comfortable with economy of motion. Get a video camera and have someone shoot you in close-up until you are able to combine the elements of stillness, focus, and relaxation.

*Extraneous movement distracts the audience from the story being told.*

*Being still is not the same as being frozen. Stillness manifests through relaxation, trust, and connection.*

*Gestures and movements must be those of the character, not those of the actor.*

## REHEARSING ON YOUR OWN

Being on the set is not like acting class. If it doesn't go well, George Clooney won't be coming over to your place to rehearse so the two of you can bring the scene back next week. In many instances, your exploration will be limited to the time it takes to light and block the scene.

Try the following exercise in your acting class: pick a scene and a partner but don't meet with them outside of class. Do all of your homework on your own. Then when you get to class, take about twenty minutes to run lines and block the scene with your partner. This will mirror the possible time frame of your on-set experience.

*When you're a big star working on big budget productions, you'll be able to do as many takes as you want. But for now, come to the set ready to nail each scene on the first take.*

## HITTING YOUR MARKS

As you rehearse the blocking (staging), notice where you wind up in relation to the other actors and the props, not just the marks on the floor. After the blocking has been set, there'll be a break so they can set up the camera and lights. Take a minute or two to go over the blocking on your own until you can hit your marks at performance speed without having to consciously think about them. Then when it comes time to shoot, you can focus on your character's circumstances, not hitting your marks.

Here's an exercise to practice at home or in your acting class: pick a short scene, set up marks around the space and repeat your movements until you can do the blocking without thinking about it.

*Justify the blocking for your character so you have a logical reason for each of your movements. Otherwise, it will look like you're going from point A to point B because you were told to.*

## SHOOTING OUT OF SEQUENCE

Film is generally shot in the order that is most economical and convenient to the production. For example, in a love story, the scene where you first make love might be shot before the scene where you first meet. Your job is to work out the arc of your character's entire story before you begin filming, so you always know where you're coming from, literally as well as emotionally. Take detailed notes for each scene so you can see exactly what your character has gone through to reach this point in the script (whether the previous scenes have been shot or not).

*Work out the arc of the character's entire story so you always know where you're coming from, literally as well as emotionally.*

## READING OFF-CAMERA

If the other actor is shooting her close-up and you're reading off-camera, make sure to give her plenty to react to. If you do, it's more likely she'll reciprocate when the camera comes around for your close-up. But, if it's a big emotional scene and they're shooting the other actor first, it's a good idea to hold back just a tiny bit so you don't do all of your best work off-camera. Save that little bit extra for your own close-up.

# LETTING THE OTHER ACTOR RUIN YOUR CLOSE-UP

You were taught in acting class to really listen and play off what the other actor is giving you. But what do you do if the other actor doesn't give you very much to react to? If it's a scene of conflict, you might blame the other actor through the author's words, allowing your genuine feelings of frustration, anger, and disappointment to flow through the material. If it's a scene where you're supposed to have positive feelings, you might imagine your partner is too shy to reveal his true self and your character is trying to draw him out. Alternatively, your most effective course of action may be to just focus on the words and not how they're being delivered.

*Attribute any weakness the other actor may have to the character he is playing and the situation the two of you are in. That way you can turn any acting problem into an opportunity to make each moment even more genuine and organic.*

# BACKWARDS AND FORWARDS

You may think you know your lines, but performing on a set with an actual director, cast, crew, cameras and lights is a totally different experience. If you're an unseasoned actor, you may be feeling a lot of pressure and the first thing to go out of your head may be your dialogue. To avoid this potential problem, run your lines with friends, family members, and other actors until you know them backwards and forwards. That way when you're actually on the set, you'll have one less thing to be concerned about.

## WHAT'S MY LINE?

If you forget your lines while the camera is rolling, stay in character and keep your attention on your partner. Take a deep breath and notice how beautiful your partner looks or try to count your partners nose hairs. It'll seem like hours have past, but in actuality it'll only be a split second. Most of the time the lines will come back to you.

Forgetting your lines may be evidence that you're letting go of control and having a genuine emotional moment. It might be your subconscious raising your work to the next level. Go with it. The worst thing that will happen is the director will say cut and you'll do another take.

## ACTION/CUT

Only the director can start the scene by calling action and only the director can stop the scene by yelling cut. If you forget your line, miss your mark, or the other actor gives you the wrong cue, you still have to stay fully involved in the scene. The director may see something spontaneous happening that she really likes. You never know.

**Note:** If you are in danger of being injured or hurting someone else, it's appropriate to step out of the scene.

*The emotional life of the character doesn't end just because you're out of words. Keep your thoughts and impulses alive until the director yells cut.*

143

# WORKING WITH THE DIRECTOR

## FEEDBACK ON THE SET

If you aren't given any direction or feedback, it's because you're already doing what the director wants. Working on a movie set is not like being in acting class. There is no time for detailed discussions of what worked and what didn't work and how you felt about what you did. The director has a lot more on her mind than just your performance. She's concerned about lighting, camera movement, composition, falling behind schedule, and a million other details. If the director had to stop to reassure everyone on the set, *("Hey Bob, great job on the lighting!" "Mary, wonderful work with the focus!")* nothing would ever get done.

***Getting hired and paid may be the only feedback you ever receive. If you're a professional, that should be enough.***

***If the director leaves you alone, it's because what you're doing is working.***

**144**

## JUSTIFYING THE DIRECTION

Direction is almost always communicated in terms of desired end result. *"Pick up the pace." "More emotion." "Look away when you say that line." "Cross the room and pour yourself a drink."* Actors often incorporate the director's notes without taking a moment to justify the adjustments. Satisfying the director is necessary, but it isn't enough. Alter your intention or change your moment before to create the desired result organically. For example, if the director tells you to pick up the pace, do it because you you're bursting to tell the other character what you want and you can't wait another second, not just because the director tells you to talk faster.

*Allow the direction to compel you deeper into the character's circumstances. Don't just do it because the director told you to.*

*Direction should be a springboard to action, not a straight-jacket.*

## "MY CHARACTER WOULD NEVER DO THAT"

You may know your character better than anyone else in the world, but the director is considering the entire project when she tells you what she wants. Always do your utmost to make any direction you're given work. If you're confused or you have another perspective, discuss it diplomatically with the director. In most cases, time and budget permitting, she'll be receptive to your point of view.

*Your primary job as an actor is to serve and fulfill the director's vision.*

*Some directors encourage the actor's input. Others have a vision of exactly what they want and aren't interested in the actor's perspective. Your best course of action is to remain flexible and receptive in either case.*

*The more the actor brings to the role, the better it makes the director look.*

## DIRECTING THE OTHER ACTORS

There's only one director and if it isn't you, don't tell the other actors how to play their parts. If another actor asks your opinion, tender your advice judiciously or else politely refer them to the director. They may want reassurance more than a critique.

*If you give another actor direction, are you willing to take the blame if it doesn't work?*

## NITPICKING YOUR PERFORMANCE TO DEATH

When you finish shooting a scene and you hear the assistant director shout, *"Moving on!"* assume they got what they needed. Actors have a tendency to waste a lot of time beating themselves up because they didn't do the scene the way they thought they should have. It's o.k. to take a few minutes to review your performance, but then let it go. You may think your work was mediocre, only to be pleasantly surprised when you eventually view your performance.

# THE CREW

## THE SCRIPT SUPERVISOR

Part of the script supervisor's (continuity person) job is to make sure your movements and dialogue match from take to take so the editor will be able to cut the film. But since the script supervisor has a lot more to worry about than just your performance, here are three things to be aware of:

1. If you're sipping a drink, scratching your nose, or fiddling with your hair, you'll have to sip, scratch, and fiddle at the same point during each take, so keep those types of actions to a minimum (unless they are specific aspects of the character's physicality). Otherwise, your focus will be on repeating your behavior rather than dealing with what's really going on in the scene.
2. If you're not sure of your exact movements in the previous take, ask the continuity person. He'll be able to check his notes. (They write down your specific actions within the scene.)
3. If you have a bathroom break between shots of the same scene, be sure your shirts, pants, ties, and skirts are buttoned, zippered, and tied the same way they were before the break.

## HAIR, MAKE-UP, AND WARDROBE

It's your face and body that's going to be up there on the big screen so if your appearance doesn't feel right, speak up. Suggest the adjustments you believe are necessary. Speak politely, but assertively. You were hired because of your understanding of the character. That includes "the look" of the character. In most cases, they'll be open to your suggestions, but if an agreement can't be reached, ask to speak to the director. Remember, you don't work for hair, make-up, and wardrobe. They're there to make you look as good as possible.

**Note one:** In most cases, "hair," "make-up," and "wardrobe" will discuss your character with the director before meeting with you.

**Note two:** You'll often find yourself making small talk with the hair, make-up, and wardrobe people while you're being readied. Unless it helps you to prepare, don't spend your time talking about traffic, the weather, or last night's ball game. Getting into wardrobe, hair, and make-up is your time to relax and focus. If you need to get centered, it's your responsibility to politely let them know.

**Note three:** When you have a lunch break, change out of your wardrobe or ask for an oversized shirt to cover what you're wearing so you don't pick up any jello stains that your character didn't have in earlier takes.

**Note four:** If you've been cast in a major role in a film or as a series regular on a TV show, you'll probably be meeting with the wardrobe department prior to the shoot date. If you have an idea of how your character would dress, consider bringing tear sheets (photographs) from magazines so the wardrobe people can get a clear understanding of how you think the character might dress.

**Note five:** If you're a person of color, consider bringing your own make-up and hair products with you to the shoot. (Sometimes they don't stock the items necessary for your complexion and hair.)

# DOWN TIME

If they won't be shooting your scenes for several hours, take advantage of your free time:

1. Without drawing attention to yourself, observe how the stars relate to and communicate with the director and each other. Watch how they rehearse their choices and explore the blocking. Figure out what it is they're doing that got them to the position you aspire to.

2. Ask a production assistant for permission to rehearse in the space they'll be shooting your scene (if it's not currently being used), so you can get comfortable in the world your character is going to inhabit. Promise you won't move anything around. Use the time to explore and discover facets of the environment you might be able to draw on when they shoot your scene. Consider ideas for blocking and creative use of props. Ask the prop department if you can work with some of the props they'll be using in your scene.

3. If there are several set-ups before your scene, don't work your role to death. Spend part of your time relaxing in your dressing room. Take a nap, read a book, meditate, stretch, do some deep breathing, have a light snack, phone a friend, or listen to music on your walkman.

4. Ask a P.A. (production assistant) to let you know when they begin to set up the scene prior to yours. This will allow you plenty of time to prepare, but not enough time to leave your best takes in the dressing room.

## WHERE'D YOU GO?

Make sure the second A.D. or P.A. know where you are at all times. Even if you've been told you have three or four hours until you next scene, they might change their minds and switch the order or decide to stick you in a scene you weren't originally in.

## GETTING HIRED AGAIN AND AGAIN

Develop the mindset that the current project is only the first of many collaborations with this director, producer, and film company. Not only do you want to do great work and demonstrate how easy you are to work with, but you also want to lay the groundwork to be thought of for future projects. Without making a pest of yourself, take advantage of down time to develop relationships with your fellow filmmakers. Then make sure you have a way to keep in touch (e-mail, regular mail, telephone) so you can stay on top of what they have in development, as well as letting them know what projects you're currently working on.

**Note:** If the industry people are busy or don't seem receptive, don't be intrusive. You'll be doing more harm than good. Just let the work speak for itself

*Your goal is to work for the industry people you meet, not just once, but again and again.*

## POST-PRODUCTION

Sometimes there is a technical glitch during the actual shoot and some of your dialogue may need to be re-recorded after filming is completed. In post-production, you'll be instructed to loop your lines into a microphone while watching your performance on the big screen. It's important to match the dialogue with your mouth movement, but even more important to retain the quality of your original performance. Too often, actors focus only on getting the words to sync with their mouth movement and forget about what's happening emotionally in the scene. To avoid this mistake, do the same degree of preparation you did when you originally shot the scene.

**Note:** Bring your original script with all of your notes to post-production. That way you can prepare the same way you did for the actual shoot.

*The sound people will be happy if the looping matches but that won't be enough to please the audience and it shouldn't be enough to please you.*

## PRACTICING YOUR CAMERA TECHNIQUE

In most cities, your local cable provider is required by statute to make studio space and broadcast time available to the general public at little or no cost. Public access cable is a great way to practice your on-camera skills (and maybe even get film on yourself). Call your local cable provider and ask for the public access department. They'll tell you the steps you need to take to use their facilities. Once you've completed the process, you'll be assigned a director and crew to work with in a three camera facility. You'll be able to bring in other actors to shoot scenes, monologues, improvisations, or anything else you can think of. You can even tell them what day and time to air your show. It's the best deal in town.

*If your competition is working harder than you are, they're a step closer to having what you say you want.*

# EXTRA WORK

## PROS OF DOING EXTRA WORK

1. If you get three SAG (Screen Actors Guild) vouchers while doing extra work, you are eligible to join the union.

2. If you are good at networking, you can develop contacts on the set.

3. If you are observant and unobtrusive you can learn a lot about the filmmaking process, so when you do get cast in a principle role, you'll already be comfortable working on a set.

4. Would you rather spend your days on a movie set or waiting tables?

5. If you hustle you can easily pay your bills. The base pay for SAG TV and film extra work is one hundred dollars for an eight hour day and the overtime pay rate is even higher.

6. The base pay for extra work on commercials is two hundred seventy five dollars for an eight hour day. It's not unheard of for an extra to be upgraded to a principle role, thereby receiving residual checks every time the commercial airs.

7. If you earn enough you can get free medical coverage for a full year.

8. You have scheduling flexibility. If you don't want to work on a particular day, just don't call in your availability to the extra casting people.

9. You may be kept waiting for several hours before you are called to the set. Think of it as being paid to use your time creatively. Bring a laptop computer and write a screenplay; e-mail your loved ones; trade stocks on line; learn your lines for acting class; meditate; knit an afghan; listen to self-help or dialect tapes on your walkman.

10. If you're a background player, you can still create a character with a specific walk, thought process, and objective.

11. The bottom line: extra work is like everything else in life. You can make the most of it or the least of it. It's up to you.

## CONS OF DOING EXTRA WORK

1. In most cases, doing extra work leads to more extra work.

2. If you are hoping to get upgraded, you should be aware that in almost all cases, principle speaking roles have been cast prior to the day of the shoot.

3. Some casting people will not read you for a speaking part once they know you do extra work. (In almost all cases, the only way they'll ever find out you do extra work is if you tell them.)

4. If you're trying to get an agent, putting extra work on your resume won't help. Agents are looking for people they can turn into stars, not people who blend into the background.

5. Background players are often treated like second class citizens. Their comfort level is not a priority and in many cases they are strongly warned not to speak to or even make direct eye contact with the "stars."

6. In many cases, extra work consists of nothing more complicated than walking past the principle players while pretending to speak. You have to leave your ego at the door.

*Extra work is like everything else in life. You can make the most of it or the least of it. It's up to you.*

# SITCOM SINS & SECRETS

## DUMP LOGIC AND HONESTY

In the world of the sitcom character, the qualities of insecurity, immaturity, and selfishness rule. Logic, honesty, and integrity have no place because they don't create conflict and they aren't funny. If you can embrace the idea of being a big selfish jerk (George Castanza from "Seinfeld"), a well-meaning moron ("Gomer Pyle"), an insincere smartass (David Spade from "Just Shoot Me"), or a pompous, insecure snob ("Frazier"), you will be welcomed into this arena with open arms.

*Sitcom characters are needy, greedy, immature and insecure. If you can embrace these qualities you'll have it made.*

*Sitcom characters love being miserable and they love sharing their misery with everyone around them.*

*If you find the flaws, you'll find the character.*

## CHILDREN IN ADULT BODIES

Sitcom humor comes from the divergence between the chronological and the emotional age of the character. For example, Danny DeVito's character, Louis DePalma on "Taxi," seemingly an adult, is actually a mischievous brat wreaking havoc on everyone with whom he comes in contact. Lucille Ball from "I Love Lucy"

155

is really a naughty little girl getting into trouble with her best friend, Ethel. Lucy's "daddy" Ricky punishes her when he gets home from work and she cries like a baby. The entire cast of "Friends," although played by adults, are in effect confused adolescents in the throes of puberty. The elderly parents on most sitcoms are big surly babies needing constant attention. The children on sitcoms are often the real adults, observing and criticizing their parents' immature behavior.

*Sitcom characters are like children. They have short attention spans and they think the world revolves around them.*

*At the end of the show, there's usually a scene where the characters suddenly grow up and forgive each other for behaving so immaturely. But sure enough, next week they're back to being children.*

## FREAKING OUT

Sitcom characters are more likely to freak out over a broken fingernail or having a big butt than getting shot at. They are more likely to be distraught over the death of a pet turtle than the demise of a spouse. Watch George, Elaine, Jerry, and Kramer on "Seinfeld." The premise and success of the show hinges on their overreactions to and obsessions with each of the trivial occurrences in their lives.

*If they have a choice of lying or telling the truth, sitcom characters always lie.*

156

*Sitcoms characters always think they're right and everyone else is wrong.*

*Sitcom characters only exist in the highlights of a world lasting 22 minutes a week (30 minutes minus 8 minutes of commercials). Therefore, every single moment must be explored fully to maximize its impact.*

*Sitcom characters are committed to their points of view, even if it kills them or everyone around them.*

## OVER THE TOP

Going "over the top" means being extreme and outrageous. It doesn't mean being fake or phony. Your work must still be grounded in reality even if you're directed to go bigger. *"But I would never react that way in real life."* Really? If, in your real life, you got a bad haircut, would you say, *"Oh well. No big deal. It'll grow out in a few weeks?"* Of course not! You would rant and rave, scrutinize yourself in the mirror from every angle, hide your hair under a hat and assume people on the street were staring at you. Your reactions would be extreme, but real. It's no different when you're doing a sitcom. If you personalize the material and raise the stakes you may go "over the top," but you'll still be authentic.

*When sitcom characters are unhappy, they're miserable. When they're happy, they're ecstatic.*

## SET YOUR VCR/TIVO

It's very difficult to absorb the rhythm, pacing, and style if you don't watch sitcoms. Just watching "Friends" isn't enough. You must be familiar with every sitcom. And not just the new ones. Why do you think the classics have been re-running for the last thirty years? There's a musicality to the writing that is easily mastered through consistent viewing. In addition, you'll see that the inspiration for almost every current sitcom character is an earlier sitcom character. Archie Bunker from "All in the Family" is a bigoted version of Ralph Kramden from "The Honeymooners." Kramer from "Seinfeld" is an manic off-shoot of Reverend Jim from "Taxi." Dharma from "Dharma and Greg" is a new age version of "Lucy." "Sabrina the Teenage Witch" is a hipper version of Samantha from "Bewitched." How can this help you? TV is a derivative medium (a nice way of saying they steal from themselves). Whatever worked well last week is what they'll be looking to replicate this week. By immersing yourself in these shows, you'll learn to incorporate pacing, delivery, and rhythm in your own work.

*There's a musicality to sitcoms. The best way to learn the notes and master the rhythms is to study sitcoms already on the air.*

*Your job is to figure out what the actors on sitcoms are doing to make millions of people want to watch them every week.*

## THE HUMOR OF OPPOSITES

Characters often say one thing and then instantaneously blurt out the opposite. *"I love you so much. I just eloped with your sister." "This is the best meal I've ever had. I think I'm going to be sick."* The second sentence is delivered in a way that completely retracts the first (blurted out, muttered, shouted or whispered, very quickly without a pause). The key is to commit to each moment as it happens. That way you won't anticipate the second sentence while you're saying the first.

*Like small children, sitcom characters go from one emotional extreme to another instantaneously.*

## FUNNY IS AS FUNNY DOES

Lucille Ball was considered to be one of the greatest comedians of all time. Guess what? She has said that she didn't think she was funny. Not only that, but she wasn't even trying to be funny. What she was doing was making strong interesting choices. She decided to let other people worry about whether she was funny or not.

*Your primary focus has to be going after what your character wants, not trying to be funny.*

## AUDIENCE LAUGHTER

If you hold for the audience laughter before it happens (because you know the joke is coming), you'll take the audience out of the scene. Concentrate on listening and staying connected to your partner so the audience laughter can surprise you into waiting before delivering your next line.

*If you're anticipating the laughter, you're watching the show. You aren't in it.*

## CUTTING THE LAUGHTER SHORT

Think of the audience laughter like a wave in the ocean. Let it grow as large as it can. When it starts to decline, ride over it to deliver your next line.

*Audience laughter is the payment for all your hard work. Don't cut it off prematurely.*

## RELYING ON THE DIALOGUE

You can get as big a laugh from your nonverbal reactions, gestures, and behavior as you can from the dialogue.

## AD-LIBBING

The writers are getting paid a lot of money to put the words in your mouth. You'll make them very happy if you say them exactly as written.

## "BIT" PLAYER"

In most cases if you have a "bit" part, you're there to feed the set-up line to the star so he or she can get the big laugh. In effect, you're passing the ball to Michael Jordan so he can dunk it and get the glory. You are an important part of the team, just not the hero.

## TENSION ON THE SET

Some sets are relaxed. Some are uptight. If there is tension, it probably existed long before you came along and it will still be there after you leave. Don't waste your time even thinking about it. Focus on the work and keep an emotional distance from anything that fails to contribute to your playing fully in the moment.

***Don't let negative energy determine the quality of your work.***

# ONE CAMERA VS. FOUR CAMERAS

In a four camera sitcom (shot in front of a live audience), the performances tend to be somewhat bigger than one camera shows which are shot without audience reaction. These parameters must be considered when you're auditioning so you can adjust the size of your performance to the style of show you're reading for.

# ADDING "UMMS" AND "YA KNOWS"

The pacing in sitcoms is fast and furious. Unnecessary pauses, speaking too slowly, adding extraneous "umms" and "ya knows" throw off everyone's timing. The dialogue must be delivered smoothly and cleanly, without hesitation.

# WHO'S THE BOSS?

The real power in sitcoms is held by the writer/producer, not the director. In many cases the director is a glorified traffic cop. *"Move there." "Throw that line away." "Pick up the pace."* Treat the director with the utmost respect by incorporating any notes you're given, but if you receive any direct input from the writer/producer, that should take precedence.

## THE TABLE READ

A table read for a sitcom is not like a table read for a play where you may have weeks to rehearse. At a sitcom table read there will be producers and network executives who are unfamiliar with you and your work. Whatever they see you do is all they will assume you are capable of. Therefore, they must see your best work now. Do the same level of work at the table read as you did to get the part; as close to a finished performance as possible (without the blocking).

## THE SERIES REGULARS

If you are a day player or a guest star on a TV show, do not adopt the sometimes casual manner of the series regulars. They may be indulged if they show up late or don't know their lines or think the story line is lame or joke around before a take. If you're a guest star and you behave this way, you will be replaced.

**Note:** Most series regulars are motivated and have good work habits.

## REWRITES AND CUTS

It isn't unusual for a script to be completely rewritten during the rehearsal process. There are several possible reason for this to happen, most of which have nothing to do with you.

1. The writer/producers have heard the material so many times that it's no longer funny to them so they rewrite it or cut it.

2. The writer/producers get paid a lot of money to tinker with the script so they rewrite it. Whether their changes make the script better or not is a matter of opinion.

3. The episode is running long.

4. Even though your lines are getting laughs, your story line is superfluous.

5. The star of the show expects to get the laugh so they rewrite the scene to give her the punchline.

6. You've gotten a big laugh every time you've delivered a particular line, but now you're anticipating the joke or imitating what you did during an earlier run-through. If you have a strong moment before, a solid objective and you really listen, this won't be the reason for the rewrite.

# SOAP OPERA MYTHS

## GETTING STUCK

Actors often hear that if they work on soap operas, they'll never be able to cross over to nighttime television and feature films. Roy Scheider, Gina Davis, Demi Moore, Ray Liotta, Julianne Moore, Alec Baldwin, Meg Ryan, Luke Perry, Kevin Bacon, Martin Sheen, Robert DeNiro, Ted Danson, Kathleen Turner, Tommy Lee Jones, Peter Falk, and Marisa Tomei are just a few of the major stars who started in soaps. Plenty of people will tell you what you can't do. It doesn't mean you have to believe them.

*Where else can you get steady work as an actor forty five weeks a year?*

*Plenty of people will tell you what you can't do. It doesn't mean you have to listen.*

## LETTING YOUR AGENTS AND MANAGERS GET LAZY

As soon as you are established on a soap, let your agents and managers know that their job is just beginning. Press them to find plays you can appear in as well as other film and TV projects that can be worked into your schedule. Push them to get you roles that show you in a very different light than the character you play on the soap. This is the time for them to lay the ground work for the future, not to rest on your laurels.

# EXPOSURE

Being on a soap is like being a politician. Hire a publicist, do charity work, and make public appearances. Create your own website so you can maintain and expand your fan base. Answer your mail or hire a service to do so. Some of the soaps actually count the amount of mail you receive to determine your popularity, which influences how long you stay on the show as well as how much you get paid. Your fan base will follow you from project to project. Don't minimize their importance.

**Note:** Consult with network or outside security about the do's and don'ts of fan relations. There will always be a small number of fans with whom you should not correspond. Your personal safety comes first.

# BAD ACTING

Unlike nighttime television where a week or more may be spent shooting a one hour show, an hour's worth of material is shot every day on a soap! Because of time constraints, the work is often result oriented with little room for subtley. You may be working with actors who've been on the show forever and seem to be "phoning it in." It may feel like all you have time to do is to learn your lines and hit your marks. Even the producers may not care about the quality of the acting as long as they wrap before they have to pay out overtime.

It's easy to get lazy and maybe no one will care or you can take advantage of the opportunity to learn to work quickly and well. Before you go on the set, take a few extra minutes to give your character a secret, a strong moment before, and some internal obstacles that serve the material but aren't spelled out in the script. Fantasize about the best and the worst things that could happen to your character in the scene. Notice, imagine, or create something about the other players in the scene that will allow you to love or hate them even more.

Continue to take acting classes or work with a coach where you can discover character elements that you may have missed on your own. Try the following exercise in your acting class: pick a scene from the show and if your character is sympathetic, do the scene as if she's the villain. If your character is unlucky in love do the scene as if she's a femme fatale. Improvise your role by blurting out everything your character would never say and doing all the things she would never do. Obviously you won't be able to do the part this way, but subtle remnants of this exercise may bleed into your character, thereby enlivening your work on the show.

Watch tapes of your work with an acting coach and review your choices in detail. Going the extra mile will help you add a depth and detail to you work that will pay off in the long run.

## IF YOUR STORY LINE IS GOING FLAT

Writers are always looking for interesting ways to use the characters on the show, but sometimes they miss the boat. If you feel your story isn't developing in a way where you're being utilized fully, don't give the writers actual plot points but do speak to them in terms of your character. *"I'm not a writer, but I feel my character is pent up and ready to explode."*

When you're in a scene with a character you're only peripherally involved with, pay a little extra non-verbal attention. Imagine a subtle sexual connection or antagonism. The writers may pick up on that energy and expand your story line

*In soaps the story is king. Without stepping on toes, make sure you do everything in your power to insure that yours is a good one.*

# SECTION FIVE:
# BREAKING FREE
# OF BARRIERS

*"I'm too thin, my teeth are crooked, and my neck is much too long," says Audrey Hepburn in "Love in the Afternoon." Gary Cooper answers, "Maybe so, but I like the way it all hangs together."*

*"No one can make you feel inferior without your consent."*
                                        -Eleanor Roosevelt

# CHANGING YOUR PERSPECTIVE

## "BUT THERE'S TOO MUCH COMPETITION"

Many well-meaning people will tell you that you're crazy for pursuing your dream; that there's too much competition; that for every part there are a thousand actors. That may be true, but what they won't tell you is that only 20% of actors are focused, disciplined, and driven. The other 80% want the rewards of success, but aren't willing to do the work. Do the math. You can eliminate eight out of ten right now. Better odds already. One last question. Which category are you in?

*"There's a lot of talent. But I think talent in the world is very ordinary, very common. There's plenty of it. However, disciplined talent is very, very rare."*
*- Irving Stone, Author.*

## REJECTION

Even if the director, producer, and casting people all agree that you read better than anyone else, you still might not get the part. Perhaps they've decided your hair is too red, or not red enough, or you have too much of it, or not enough. Maybe they just want a blonde. Maybe they think you're too tall to play opposite the actor they've already hired. Maybe they want someone who looks more intimidating or more homely. Maybe another actor has more credits on his resume or has already worked with the producer on another project. Maybe you remind the casting person of his high school gym

171

teacher, the one who made him run around the track in the rain. The point is there could be a million valid or stupid reasons why you don't get cast in a role. Auditioning for a part is not like a math test where there's only one right answer.

Acting is a profession where most of the time, no matter how brilliant you are, you're going to be turned down. Taking rejection personally is like agreeing to play football and then wondering why the other players keep trying to tackle you. As soon as you realize that it's all just part of the game, you can learn to let it go by putting your entire focus on your effort and none of it on the outcome.

The problem occurs when actors don't prepare to the best of their ability and then squelch their impulses during the actual reading. They do this, so if they get turned down, it won't hurt as much. In effect, they're rejecting themselves before anyone else can. Unfortunately, this plan usually backfires because rejection becomes a self-fulfilling prophesy. Don't let yourself go down that path. Think of the audition process as if it were a board game. Roll the dice and move your piece around the board to the best of your ability, but remember that you can't control what all the other players are going to do. When the game is over, see what you can learn and then get ready for the next one. If the rules of this game don't appeal to you, you can always switch to solitaire.

*Taking rejection personally is like agreeing to play football and then wondering why the other players keep trying to tackle you. As soon as you realize that it's all just part of the game, you can learn to let it go.*

## GIVING YOUR POWER AWAY TO
## "THE PEOPLE IN CHARGE"

A mistake actors make is to view casting people, producers, directors, and network executives as powerful, secure beings who hold all the cards. The reality is these people are as insecure as the rest of us. But because they don't need to be emotionally vulnerable for the work they do, they may appear to be more confident. And guess what? They aren't scrutinizing you as closely as you think they are.

The casting director is looking over his shoulder at the director and the producer. *"What if I give this actor a callback and she doesn't read as well for the director as she did for me? They won't blame the actor. They'll blame me." "I know this actor is great, but he doesn't have much experience. If they cast him on my recommendation and he screws up, they'll never hire me again. If they do take a chance on him and he does great, they'll take all the credit." "How come they give Academy Awards for everyone except casting directors? It's because nobody respects what we do." "Actors think they're the only ones who have to audition. They don't know the hoops we have to jump through to get a casting job."*

The director is looking over her shoulder at the producers for their approval. *"What if I give the auditioner an adjustment and he doesn't understand it? The producers will think I don't know how to communicate." "What if the hot young actor the producers forced me to hire falls flat? They'll make me the scapegoat." "What if the crew doesn't respect me? They'll goof off, we'll fall behind schedule, and the studio will yank me from the project." "If the star doesn't like my direction who do you think the producers are gonna side with?" "How come I'm still doing episodic television? All the guys I went to film school with are doing big budget features." "The producers give me notes every five minutes. They must hate what I'm doing." "I'm not a director. I'm a traffic cop."*

The producer is looking over her shoulder at the studio and the network. *"They promised my show a good time slot and now they've buried me on Saturday night when my target audience is out partying." "Why didn't they pick up my show after they told me how much they loved my pilot?" "They don't promote my show enough. We'll be canceled in thirteen weeks." "If the show doesn't last long enough to go into syndication, I'll lose my shirt." "The network made the star of the show my co-producer. If he doesn't like me, who do you think the network is going to fire?" "I spend all my time pitching story ideas. What if they like my idea, but they don't like me? They can just give my idea to another producer. If I complain I'll get a bad reputation and no one in town will work with me." "We're getting a lot of bad press about the star's off screen behavior. If he goes into rehab one more time, they'll cancel my show."*

What about the networks? Each year they lose more and more of their audience to cable, the internet, video games, and DVDs. As recently as 20 years ago "the big three" (CBS, NBC, & ABC) held 90% of the audience. Now if viewership tops 50%, it's cause for celebration. The networks spend millions of dollars shooting pilots, 90% of which are so bad that they'll never air. Almost all the shows that do make it to prime time are canceled before the first season is over. When you read for a series regular role, there may be up to twenty network executives watching you. If they seem cold and unfriendly it's because they know that (a) only one or two of them have the power to decide who to hire and the rest are just window dressing and (b) their opinions on who and what audiences will respond to are no more valid than yours or mine.

The bottom line is you'll be reading for and working with people who've had some successes and some failures, just like the rest of us. So the next time you audition or get an acting job, have a little empathy. If the industry people seem distant or unfriendly it probably has nothing to do with you. The reality is they're scrambling to cover their asses, just like the rest of us.

## IS THERE MORE DRAMA IN YOUR LIFE THAN IN YOUR ACTING?

*"My boyfriend ran off with his scene partner." "My girlfriend stole all the money out of my checking account." "They towed my car." "I forgot to pay the phone bill." "The battery in my pager died so I missed my callback." "My landlord called the cops because the music got too loud." "I couldn't make it to class because I was too bummed out."*

Everyone's life is chaotic once in a while, but if yours is a non-stop soap opera, you need to clean up your act. If you don't, you won't have the time to give your career the attention it deserves. If you can't straighten out your life by yourself, get some help from a therapist, a life coach, a minister, a family member, or a friend. If you think you're going to "make it" and then get your shit together, think again.

*Save the drama for your work. Make your life as focused and as disciplined as possible.*

## SHOOTING YOURSELF IN THE FOOT

Some actors find a way to sabotage each and every opportunity that comes their way, e.g. they don't prepare the way they should; they're habitually late; they denigrate the material; they fumble with dialogue they knew perfectly well at home; they give the impression that they're too good to be auditioning; they're always fighting with the director. The bottom line is no matter how talented you are, if you don't believe you deserve to be successful, you'll always find a way to undermine your chances.

Try the following exercise. Fill in the blank for each sentence. Don't edit yourself. Just write down the first thought that pops into your head.

I believe if I succeed.......
I believe if I fail.......
I believe if I let the world see how talented I really am.......
I believe if I don't make it.......
The thing that scares me about success is.......
The thing that scares me about failure is.......
In my family to be successful meant.......
I believe if I succeed my family will.......
I believe if I succeed my friends will.......
I believe if I fail my family will.......
I believe if I fail my friends will.......
My mother's beliefs about her own success were.......
My father's beliefs about his own success were.......
In school, when it came to my own success.......
When I think of my past.......
When I think of my future.......
My parents taught me that the world.......

When I was growing up, if someone in my family was successful, everyone else.......

When I sabotage my opportunities.......

When I was growing up, if one of my friends was successful I felt.......

When I hear about other actors succeeding I believe.......

The people who stand out.......

I believe if I let myself have what I really want.......

I believe if I'm successful and I get a lot of attention.......

I believe someone deserves to succeed if they.......

I believe I deserve to succeed if I.......

Review what you've written. If your responses regarding success are negative, what you learned from your parents, siblings, peers, and teachers isn't helping you. Therefore, you have two choices. You can either perpetuate those teachings by continuing to sabotage your opportunities or you can adopt a new set of beliefs by seeking out new teachers.

Make a list of all the people you consider to be successful. If you know them personally, ask them what they were taught about success. If they were ever guilty of self-sabotage, find out what did they do to get out of their own way. If the people whose achievements you admire are celebrities to whom you have no access, read every book, newspaper, and magazine article written about the paths they took and the obstacles they overcame. If you can learn to see the world the way they do and to take the actions they took, there's no reason you can't have what they have.

***It's very hard to achieve success if you don't feel you deserve it.***

*When you were a small child, you might have believed there was a monster hiding under the bed. When you eventually drew up the courage to take a look, you saw there was nothing waiting to get you. If you look inside yourself, you'll learn there is no monster keeping you from success. It's only what you were taught to believe.*

## CRITICISM

When you're acting, you want what the other actor is saying and doing to affect you on a deep emotional level. The mistake actors make is to take in criticism the same way. It's best to examine criticism intellectually before you take it in emotionally. Otherwise, the criticism can do more harm than good by causing you unnecessary emotional pain and turmoil.

Here's an exercise to shift the way you accept criticism: take some deep breaths until you're completely relaxed. Now imagine yourself behind a bulletproof plexiglass (see-through) wall. Tell yourself you are completely safe behind this wall. Repeat the following statements to yourself three times, *"Nothing can harm me or even affect me without my permission." "I will only take in what I can use to help me grow as an artist."* Imagine there's a large blackboard with plenty of chalk and a great big eraser set up outside your plexiglass wall. Now recall a time you were being criticized. Remember exactly where you were, what was being said to you, and who was saying it. See this person's words literally coming at you in large block letters, but before they can reach you, see the words hitting and bouncing off your plexiglass wall onto your blackboard. Now examine these words before you take them in. Take your time. Does the feedback seem valid? More importantly, is it being communicated in a way that can help you grow? If it looks like a hurtful personal attack, come out from behind your plexiglass wall, erase the criticism from your blackboard, and rewrite it in a way that can help you expand your capabilities. If you're not sure, take a break until you can examine the words on your blackboard from a more dispassionate place. It is in your power to decide whether to lower your plexiglass barrier to take in what is being said.

Practice this exercise every day until you can make your plexiglass wall and blackboard appear instantaneously. Then the next time you're being criticized, you can examine the feedback before you take it in.

*If the feedback you receive isn't to help you grow, ask yourself what purpose it serves before you take it in.*

*"A critic is a man who knows the way but can't drive the car."*
**-Kenneth Tynan, Writer**

*"It is not the critic who counts, not the man who points out how the strong man stumbled or where the doer of deeds could have done better. The credit belongs to the man who is actually in the arena; whose face is marred by dust and sweat and blood; who strives valiantly; who errs and comes short again; who knows the great enthusiasms, the great devotions and spends himself in a worthy cause; who at the best, knows in the end the triumph of high achievement; and who at the worst, if he fails, at least fails while daring greatly, so that his place shall never be with those cold and timid souls who knew neither victory nor defeat."*
**-Theodore Roosevelt**

179

## "I'LL GET TO IT LATER"

Imagine you were running in a marathon and every time you took a step you smashed yourself in the leg with a hammer. You'd have a great excuse for losing the race! Guess what? Procrastination is like that hammer; it's the tool you use to justify not doing your best. *"Yeah, but what if I put down my hammer of procrastination, try my hardest, and I still don't win?"* That's a good point. You might not win, but if you procrastinate you're guaranteed to lose.

Take out a sheet of paper and make a list of all the benefits you receive from procrastinating. *"But there are no benefits."* Oh, really? There is certainly a sense of safety and familiarity in being stuck in the same place. You know exactly what to expect. Plus, you can spend all your time daydreaming how someday when the world magically discovers you (without any effort on your part), you can take your rightful place amongst the greatest ever. *"But change is hard."* It certainly is. It requires that dirty little "c" word, commitment, and that nasty little "e" word, effort. *"O.k., o.k., I get the point! I'll start next week, I promise."* Hey, there's no rush. You have all the time in the world. In fact, close your eyes and imagine you're eighty years old looking back on your life. See all the opportunities that passed you by because it just wasn't the right time or you didn't feel like it or you thought you'd do it tomorrow. How does it feel knowing that every time you procrastinated, your competition moved another step ahead? If you don't like this scenario, try the following: imagine you're eighty years old, looking back on your life, only this time you busted your butt and did everything in your power to make it happen. Which scenario is more likely to give you the life you desire? Please don't wait until you're eighty to find out.

*In any moment of decision the very best thing you can do is what is right. The next best thing you can do is what is wrong. The worst thing you can do is nothing.*
                    *-Theodore Roosevelt*

*What you are afraid to do is a clear indication of the next thing you need to do.*
                    *-Ralph Waldo Emerson*

*When you procrastinate you single-handedly guarantee the annihilation of your dreams.*

*The reason we procrastinate is that we're afraid to find out whether we're as good or bad as we think we are.*

*The time it takes to do something is always less than the time spent thinking about the fact that you haven't done it.*

## AUDITION ANXIETY

No matter how great your effort and diligent your preparation, if you don't learn to relax and keep things in perspective, no one will ever see what you're capable of.

The following are some exercises to deal with audition anxiety.

### EXERCISE ONE: SWEET DREAMS

Ten minutes before you go to sleep, sit down in a comfortable, quiet place and visualize the way you would like the entire audition process to play out. See yourself dressing for the audition as if you were already living the character's prior circumstances. Instead of driving to the audition, visualize yourself driving to wherever the character you are playing would be going. While you're waiting to read, see yourself as relaxed, confident, and focused. When you hear your name called, hear yourself say, *"This is going to be so much fun."* When you enter the audition room, imagine everyone is friendly and extremely happy to see you. See and feel yourself as completely grounded in your character as you say to yourself, *"I deserve to be here and I'm ready to play."* If you're reading for a comedy, imagine everyone laughing hysterically at everything you're saying. If it's a drama, imagine the casting people on the edge of their seats totally immersed in your performance. When you're finished reading, imagine the director/casting people telling you how terrific you were. As you leave the audition room think to yourself, *"I did great and I'm really pleased with my work."* Next, imagine your agent calling to say you've booked the job. Then, see yourself on the set actually doing the job. Imagine the director and the other actors telling you how wonderful you are. Hear them say they can't wait to work with you again. As you complete this visualization say to yourself, *"Either this or something even better will happen. I give up my need for control. I give up my need for approval."*

By doing this exercise right before you go to sleep, your subconscious will assist you in the creation of your desired outcome. (But remember, this visualization is an adjunct to, not a substitute for, conscious preparation a.k.a......homework.)

**Note:** Don't wait until you have an audition to practice this exercise. Every night, right before you go to sleep, visualize how you want your next day to play out.

## EXERCISE TWO: ANCHORING SUCCESS

Recall a time when you felt really good about yourself. It can be when you received special acknowledgement at school or at home; when you achieved or completed something you didn't think you were capable of; when you excelled in a sporting event; when you first realized that you loved to act; when you had a great audition; when you landed a wonderful role; when you found God; when you were generous or loving to someone; when you had a particularly wonderful time with friends or family. Now close your eyes and imagine one of these events as if it were happening right now. Use as many of your five senses as possible. Hear the people around you saying what they originally said; see the way they're looking at you; feel them embracing you; remember all the smells and sounds of that wonderful time and place. Be very specific. Even include the weather, the time of day and to the best of your recollection what you were wearing. The more details you can recall, the better. Remember the event as it actually happened, or recall it the way you wished it would have happened, or create a totally new memory from your imagination. When you really feel you're at the emotional peak of your memory, set or anchor this extraordinary feeling by putting your thumb, index, and middle finger together and silently shouting the word,"Yes!!!"

Do this exercise every day until you have a storehouse of memories conditioned to be triggered every time you put those three fingers together. Then, when you have an audition, you'll be able to carry your history of success with you into the work.

**Note:** From now on, whenever you're feeling terrific for any reason at all, put those three fingers together and silently shout,"Yes!!!"

## EXERCISE THREE: FINDING YOUR "MERYL STREEP"

Think of someone whom you imagine has the confidence that you believe is lacking within yourself. Let's say you've picked Meryl Streep. Close your eyes and silently repeat her name over and over again. Imagine breathing her energy into your body, starting at your toes, moving up slowly through your entire body until you can feel her energy and strength coursing through your veins. When you really feel it, anchor it in by putting your three fingers together, and silently shout the word,"Yes!" (see EXERCISE TWO above) If you're doing a comedy, try channeling Robin Williams or Bugs Bunny. If you need more sexual prowess, try Marilyn Monroe or Russell Crowe.

**Note:** You are finding the "Meryl Streep" (shorthand for confidence, power, talent) within you. You aren't doing an impression of Meryl Streep.

## EXERCISE FOUR: TOM CRUISE ROCK AND ROLL

A half hour before you need to dress for your audition, find a piece of hot sexy music and do your version of Tom Cruise from "Risky Business." Strip down to your underwear (or beyond) and dance around your room. While you're moving, let out the sounds that express everything you're feeling. When you're in your body and out of your head, put your three fingers together and silently shout, "Yes!" (See EXERCISE TWO above.)

## EXERCISE FIVE: SPILLING THE BEANS

If you're freaked out about an audition, call all of your friends and let them know. Describe every aspect of your fear until you get bored with your story.

**Note:** Once your anxiety is no longer a secret, its power to control you is diminished.

## EXERCISE SIX: SCALING

On a scale of one to ten, one being the least and ten being the most, how important is your health? Your loved ones? This audition? Hopefully your health and loved ones are tens. But if your audition is also a ten then you should be nervous. You are losing perspective. *"But my career is very important to me."* Great, but remember: your career is a lot more than any single audition.

## EXERCISE SEVEN: WORKING WHILE YOU WAIT

1. While you're in the waiting room, focus on your breathing. With each exhalation silently repeat the word "relax." Do this at least fifty times. Notice where in your body you're still feeling stressed. Tighten that area as much as you can. Then relax. Then tighten. Then relax.

2. Put your entire focus on an object (a lamp, a painting, a desk) in the waiting room. Study this object until you can close your eyes and recall every detail. Open your eyes, look at the object, see what you've missed, close your eyes and do it again. Do it a third time. This exercise will help to ground you in concrete reality by getting your attention off yourself.

3. Carry a small rubber ball with you. Squeeze it as hard as you can. Imagine you are transferring every ounce of your anxiety onto this rubber ball.

4. Create the place where the scene occurs. Be very specific. Use as many of your five senses as possible.

5. Bring a walkman with you and listen to music that puts you in the mood of your character.

## EXERCISE EIGHT: MONKEY IN THE MIRROR

Get to the audition early and go to the restroom. Stand with your knees slightly bent, approximately two feet apart. Slowly bend your upper torso toward the ground. Go as far over as you can without straining your back.* Stay there with your head bent toward the ground (at knee level) and slowly count to ten. Then begin to raise your upper body one vertebrae at a time until you are standing up as straight as you can. Now go to the mirror and make funny faces. Stick your tongue out, roll your eyes, put one thumb in your ear and the other in your nose and wave at yourself with your eight remaining fingers. Speak to yourself in gibberish. Pretend you're a monkey. Jump up and down, scratch yourself, and make monkey sounds (quietly). Congratulations! You've just made a monkey out of yourself. Now you don't have to worry about anyone else doing it.

*If you have a bad back, skip this part of the exercise.

## EXERCISE NINE: GREETING YOUR FANS

When you enter the audition room, in addition to seeing the casting people, imagine a good friend or a family member or an inspiring teacher is also there to greet you. Hear them say, *"You're the greatest!" "Relax and just have fun." "I know you can do it."*

Take this exercise a step further. Imagine hundreds of fans surrounding the casting people, waving big banners with your name, cheering you on, and responding with wild enthusiasm to everything you say and do.

## EXERCISE TEN: GETTING TO KNOW YOU

Imagine the people for whom you are reading, sitting on toilets, farting away, and picking their noses. Imagine them as chickens, squawking and pooping all over the carpet. If you can visualize them as big bad monsters, why not tiny headed chickens, clucking and pecking at each other?

## EXERCISE ELEVEN: REVERSE PSYCHOLOGY

Create a character that loves to audition. Work on it the same way you would work on the part of a bank robber, a business person, or a ball player. Instead of using your imagination to make yourself nervous, why not use it to create a character that is supremely confident?

# RUNNING OUT OF TIME

*"I'm getting too old." "If I don't hit now, I'll never make it."*

Actors expend a lot of energy worrying that they're running out of time. They pick up on the hype promoted by advertisers and adopted by the industry to make them feel that unless they look sixteen, they're over the hill; that they're in a race from which they're about to be disqualified.

You must think of your career as a marathon, not a hundred yard dash. Telling yourself that you're doomed to the scrap heap is no different than telling yourself that you're not tall enough, pretty enough, or ethnic enough. Your height, age, and type are things you can't control. If you're going to continue your career, you must focus your attention on things within your power: making your work as excellent as possible, networking, self-promotion, showcasing, and maintaining a positive attitude and outlook.

**Note:** see YOU'RE ONLY AS OLD AS YOU LOOK in THE BUSINESS section.

*You must not buy into the idea that you're a horse about to be put out to pasture.*

*Do not waste your time ruminating over things you can't control.*

## "THE SHOULDA', WOULDA', COULDA' BLUES"

*"I shoulda' started my career earlier." "If I had been better at networking, I woulda' kept in touch with that important director." "I coulda' landed that part if I had a better agent."*

Your job as an artist is to learn from the past, not to wallow in it. You can use the past as evidence of your hopelessness or as a springboard to new choices in the future. Transform "shoulda', woulda', coulda'" into "I shall, I will, I can," by doing it differently the next time.

*All human beings make mistakes. Successful human beings learn from theirs.*

## REVEALING EMOTIONS

If you have difficulty expressing certain emotions, you may need to look at the verbal and behavioral messages you received as a child. If you learned from your family that it wasn't o.k. to cry or to get angry or to show love, you may feel blocked from revealing these emotions in your work. The voices you've internalized from your family may stop you.

Let's look at crying, for instance. Think of all the things it meant when someone in your family cried. Was it a sign of weakness; a source of scorn; something "big boys" and "big girls" didn't do? Now ask yourself, what will it mean if you cry as an adult? What's the worst thing that can happen? Get everything down on paper. Now try the following exercise: close your eyes, put your hand over your heart and visualize yourself as the child you once were. Tell your "child-self" that no one is going to punish, shame, or judge him; that no one is going to make him feel wrong or stupid if he needs to cry. Be gentle and take your time. The last thing you want to do is to put pressure on yourself to force an emotion. If you do this visualization on a regular basis, you will soon feel safe enough to cry. (See CRYING ON CUE in the ACTING TECHNIQUE section)

Another approach is to physicalize the emotion you're having difficulty expressing. For example, if you can't express anger, take a pillow, and repeatedly smash it to the ground (without hurting yourself) as you yell and curse at the people in your life who've pissed you off. You're going to feel self-conscious at first, but with repeated effort a few minutes a day, this external manifestation of anger will soon become genuine. If you have difficulty expressing love, get a stuffed animal, gently rock it in your arms and whisper that it's o.k. to show love. Corny? Stupid? Ridiculous? Not for the child that still exists within you waiting for permission to express whatever he's feeling.

*Before you can share your emotions with the world, you must create a sense of safety, self-acceptance, and well-being.*

*If you internalized your family's values regarding money, politics and religion, what makes you think you weren't impacted by their attitude towards emotional expression?*

## MAKING A FOOL OF YOURSELF

In "Ace Ventura: Pet Detective," Jim Carrey achieved world renown for speaking through his butt cheeks, pretending to play football in slow motion while wearing a dress, and squealing like a dolphin; things most people would be embarrassed to do anywhere, let alone for the entertainment of millions. What made his work so free was that he didn't seem to care what other people thought. He was doing it for himself. But, did you know that the first time he tried stand-up comedy, he was booed off the stage? That he was so ashamed and embarrassed that he didn't try it again for two years? He only returned when he realized that going after his dream was a lot more important than protecting himself from judgment.

What's the worst thing that can happen if you make a fool of yourself? People laugh at you? Hopefully! Remember you? Certainly. Throw things? Unlikely. Burn you at the stake? Only if you really suck.

Here's an exercise you can work on in your acting class: create a character that does every ridiculous and foolish thing that you would never be caught dead trying. If you can remember it's the character you're playing that's doing and saying these foolish things and not really you, it will make this exercise easier.

*You can't be brilliant and play it safe at the same time.*

*Once you can embrace making a fool out of yourself, nothing can stop you.*

*What's more important? Getting what you want or protecting yourself from judgment?*

# WHO'S RUNNING THE SHOW?

## LAZINESS

*"If only I had worked harder, I could have done a lot better." "I know I'm talented. I just didn't put in the time and effort." "What if I try as hard as I can and I still don't achieve my goal? I would have invested all that time and energy and not have anything to show for it. Wouldn't that be worse than not trying at all?"*

Blaming your situation on laziness is a great way to rationalize set-backs and disappointments. It protects you from ever having to fulfill your potential and as an added bonus you never have to work up a sweat! There is one question you must ask yourself. Are you satisfied with what being lazy has allowed you to accomplish? If so, keep it up. The epitaph on your tombstone can say, "Here lies someone who had a lot of potential, but unfortunately she was just plain lazy."

*"O.K., I admit I'm lazy. Should I just quit right now?"* First of all, laziness is not an incurable disease or an inborn condition. It's a learned behavior. So how did you learn to be lazy? Did a parent, teacher, or sibling stick that label on you? Were they trying to motivate you? Did it work or was it easier just to agree with them? Perhaps you worked really hard on something and were disappointed with the result; did you decide that next time you wouldn't bother trying so hard? When you were younger maybe everything came easily to you, so you never learned to put in the effort. The bottom line is, if you learned to be lazy you can learn to work hard.

## THREE STEPS TO OVERCOMING LAZINESS

1. Select a disappointing experience from your past where laziness might have been a contributing factor. Close your eyes and imagine this event unfolding as if it were on a giant movie screen. Observe it in slow motion. Ask yourself what you might have done differently to increase the likelihood of a more favorable outcome. When the movie is over, watch it again, only this time imagine yourself working hard and having the event turn out the way you would have liked. Re-run your edited movie three times in slow motion, five times at normal speed, then ten timcs as fast as you can. Remember, the past only exists in your imagination. You can use it as a learning tool or a life sentence. It's your choice.

2. Create a character with the following attributes: an extremely talented actor with the energy and motivation to do everything necessary to accomplish her goals. As part of your preparation make a list of all the actions you imagine this character would take to achieve her desired outcome. Work on this role every waking hour for the next week. If you don't like playing this part, you can always go back to playing the role of a couch potato.

3. Take out a sheet of paper and draw a straight line.

On a scale of one to ten, one being a lazy bum and ten being super-motivated, where do you fall? If you're at a two, what action would you need to take to raise yourself to a three? Take that action right now. To a four? Do it next. To a five?....... etc.

1____2____3____4____5____6____7____8____9____10
lazy bum                  average                super

*If the key to a door doesn't fit, find another key or another door or knock the door down or climb in through a window. If you just stand there and bang your head against the door, the only thing you'll get is a headache.*

*Being lazy makes the likelihood of failure a self-fulfilling prophesy.*

*Everyday you must ask yourself, "What will I do today to advance my career?"*

## BEATING YOURSELF UP

*"Why can't I get it right?" "Why am I such a loser?" "What gives me the right to even call myself an actor?" "I really made a fool of myself this time." "I can't believe I made the same stupid mistake again." "Who do I think I am? I should quit right now. I'm wasting my life." " My parents were right. I'll never amount to anything." "I'm just fooling myself."*

Sound familiar? If, despite your best efforts, you've suffered a setback, you're probably already feeling badly about yourself. It makes no sense to beat up on yourself at precisely the time you need the most love and support.

Imagine you had a child who came home from school having done poorly on an assignment. Would you tell your child what a loser she was? That she'd never amount to anything? Would you threaten to disown her? Of course not! You would brainstorm ways to improve for the next time. You would tell her that you loved her and as long as she did the best she could, you would always be proud of her. This is precisely what you need to tell yourself when your efforts haven't been as successful as you would have hoped.

If you go out in the world with your fist balled up, ready to beat yourself, how can you possibly feel confident enough to do your best work? If you had a friend who had experienced the same setback you had, would you tell her that she stunk? That she should go dig a hole and hide there for the rest of her life? Of course not! If your friend deserves to be treated with love and respect, why don't you?

Ask yourself, if beating yourself up, helps you do your best work. If the answer is no, then what do you have to lose by trying constructive feedback and positive loving self-talk? Of course, it's much "cooler" to beat the shit out of yourself. But guess what? It ain't working.

*"I did the best I could with the tools I had at the time." "Let's figure out where I went off so I can nail it the next time." "I think I need to do more work on my prior circumstances." "Some of my choices worked, but I need to do more with my opening beats." "I didn't do as well as I'd hoped, but I know what to work on for next time." "I'm not sure where I went off. I'll have to give it some thought."*

*In many cases beating yourself up is so habitual, you're not even aware that you're doing it.*

## NEGATIVE SELF-TALK

Many actors have negative inner voices that never let up. It's like having their worst nightmare of a teacher, parent, or bully chewing them out twenty-four hours a day. The theory is, if the actor kicks his own ass before anyone else can, he'll be prepared for whatever the world has in store for him. In reality, the only thing negative self-talk is guaranteed to accomplish is to make the actor feel miserably insecure.

If you recognize this pattern within yourself, the following are some steps to lessen the power of your critical voice:

1. Give your negative voice a name. Choose one that you can't possibly take too seriously or be overly respectful of. How bout "Bratty," "Silly Billy," "Chatty Cathy," or "Schmo?"
2. Give "Bratty" a silly voice so whatever he says will sound ridiculous; e.g. try Mickey Mouse's voice or Elmer Fudd's or Porky Pig's.
3. Take out a pen and paper and transcribe everything "Bratty" (who sounds amazingly like Porky Pig) has to say for a full half hour.
4. After a half hour put down your pen, and thank "Bratty" for his input. Read your pages over to see if there's anything he's said that can improve your life or make you a better actor. Set those pages aside, rip up the rest, toss them in the garbage can, and thank "Bratty" for his efforts.
5. Let "Bratty" know that you'll listen to whatever he has to say the same time every day for a full half hour.
6. If "Bratty" starts up again during the course of the day, remind him that he's already had his half hour and he'll have to save his "brilliant" insight until tomorrow. Let "Bratty" know that if he doesn't behave himself, he won't even get a half hour.

Your goal is not to get rid of your critical voice, but to reduce the power it wields. Otherwise, it's like allowing a two year old having a temper tantrum to run your life and then wondering why you feel so miserable.

**Note:** If a half hour a day isn't enough time, start with an hour a day, and if possible, work your way down to fifteen minutes.

*The major thing negative self-talk accomplishes is to stop you from achieving your dreams.*

## THE PROBLEM WITH PERFECTION

If being a perfectionist motivates you to do your best work, then by all means keep it up. Unfortunately, most perfectionists give themselves a convenient excuse to quit because they know they'll never meet the impossible standards they set for themselves. The process itself brings them little pleasure because all that matters is the outcome.

In the dramatic arts, what one person may think of as perfect another may dismiss as mediocre. In addition, the most memorable characters are flawed and the flaws are what makes them fascinating to watch. Therefore, if you want to do wonderful work, focus on finding your character's Achilles heel, rather than trying to be perfect.

*"Perfectionism is not a quest for the best, it is a pursuit of the worst in ourselves, the part that tells us nothing we do will ever be good enough. "*
*- Julia Cameron, <u>The Artist's Way</u>*

*Strive for excellence, not perfection.*

## YOUR BANK ACCOUNT AND RESUME

Many actors are unwilling to think of themselves as "real actors" because they haven't made it yet. They're concerned that if they tell people that they're actors, but they haven't appeared in anything of note, they'll be judged and put down. Their concerns about other people's opinions is a reflection of their own self-doubt.

If you nurture your talent and do everything in your power to make it happen, then you are worthy of calling yourself an actor. As soon as you realize this, you'll actually begin to work more because you won't be putting so much pressure on yourself every time you go out there. You'll realize that auditioning and performing are opportunities to play, not pressure-filled situations to prove to the world that you're worthy of being in the game.

*Tell everyone you meet that you're an actor. Shout it from the mountain tops. Not because the world needs to hear it, but because you do.*

## "BUT I DON'T HAVE AN AGENT"

You must own your talent and your right to call yourself an actor, whether you have representation or not. Who and what you are must not be contingent on other people's validation and acceptance. That holds true not just for agents, but for casting people, producers, and directors. If you're waiting to sign with an agent before you feel worthy of calling yourself an actor, you're putting the cart before the horse. An agent represents who you already are, not who you hope she's going to turn you into.

# NOW LOOK AT ME!

Actors sometimes turn to plastic surgery to enhance their marketability and increase their confidence. Ask yourself some important questions before choosing this option.

1. What do you hope to gain professionally? Personally?
2. How will you feel it you have the surgery, but your life doesn't change?
3. Are you aware that in many cases, plastic surgery leads to more plastic surgery?
4. Is it possible you'll be eliminating what is positively unique about your appearance?
5. Have you spoken to other people who've had it done? How has it impacted their lives?
6. If you don't feel good about yourself now, what makes you think you'll feel good about yourself afterwards?
7. Are you able to accurately assess your appearance or do you tend to exaggerate and magnify the flaws you perceive?
8. If you're considering breast enhancement, would a push-up or padded bra accomplish the same thing?
9. If you're considering breast enhancement, is it because it will make you feel sexier or more of a woman? Are there things you could change about your relationship with yourself that might accomplish the same thing?
10. Are you ignoring your insides to focus on your outsides?

## COMPLIMENTS

In Hollywood they give out compliments like doggy treats. They don't cost very much and you're hungry a few minutes later. Compliments can be intoxicating, but in many cases they're a consolation prize for not getting the job. Don't misunderstand. There's nothing wrong with compliments. They can help keep you going, but take them with a grain of salt.

*Your goal is to get a job, not a compliment.*

# STARDOM

## WHAT MAKES YOU SPECIAL?

Do you believe you are special? So special that people are going to drive over to the movie theater and fork over ten bucks to stare at your face on the big screen? That the highlight of their day is going to be plopping down in front of the TV after a hard day's work to spend an hour watching you? You'd better have a pretty high opinion of yourself. Not arrogance or conceit, but a genuine awareness of what is special about you. Not only is it o.k. to feel this way, it's mandatory!

Take out a pen and paper and make a list of all the things that make you special. Need help? Ask your friends what qualities drew them to you when you first met. Ask your acting teacher and the other students in your class. Ask your family. Ask everyone you know. Write everything down on your list. Everyday, spend five minutes slowly reading this list out loud as you look at yourself in the mirror. Do this exercise until every ounce of your being tells you that it's true: you are special and you deserve to be seen by the world.

*Thinking you're special is not a conceit, but a necessity!*

*You must decide whether you're going to be one of the millions watching the chosen few or one of the chosen few being watched by millions.*

*Whatever you believe about yourself is what the rest of the world will confirm.*

## WHAT MAKES SOMEONE A STAR?

Stars aren't always the most beautiful or talented people, but they do have one thing in common. When they enter a room or pop up on the screen, we can't take our eyes away. Is it something they were born with or is it a gift that can be acquired? Let's find out. Do the following exercise every day for five minutes: close your eyes and take a few slow, deep, calming breaths. Imagine a radiant beam of light beginning to swirl around your body until it surrounds you from head to toe. Imagine that beam of light is encircled by a magnetic force field so powerful that whenever you enter a room all eyes turn towards you, drawn to your powerful, magical presence. Feel this force of energy growing stronger with each breath you take as it radiates from every pore, inch, and ounce of your being. As you do this visualization, say the words, *"I share my gifts with the world."* Then, the next time you go into read or shoot a scene, repeat those words and you'll feel a powerful positive energy flowing from you to everyone with whom you come in contact.

***Stars aren't always the most beautiful or talented actors but they do have one thing in common. When they enter a room or pop up on the screen you can't take your eyes away.***

# THE SECRETS TO BEING LUCKY

If you weren't lucky enough to have been born into a famous family, or to be drop dead gorgeous, or to have an angel watching over you, you might just have to make your own luck.

1. The harder you work, the luckier you'll get.
2. Make the most of every opportunity, and when there aren't any, create your own.
3. Ask the "lucky people" you know, to what do they owe their success? You'll be surprised how many of them made their own luck.
4. Be in the right place at the right time. And if you don't know where that is, put yourself in as many places as possible, until one of those places turns into the right place at the right time.
5. If something you're doing isn't helping you get what you want, stop doing it and do something else instead.
6. Believe you deserve good things to happen to you.

# FAME AND FORTUNE

Stop a thousand people on the street and ask them if they'd like to be actors. Who wouldn't? It's glamorous. It's exciting. You get to travel all over the world, attend big movie premieres, make barrels of money, get on the cover of People Magazine, and go on rides at Disneyland without having to wait on line. It's like winning the lottery, only better! Parents, friends and teachers who thought you'd never amount to anything, will worship the ground you walk on. You can show them all!

The reality is being famous may give you a thrill for a little while but being gawked at by millions of strangers gets old pretty fast. If your goal is to make a lot of money, there are a hell of a lot of easier ways to go about it. Even if you prove to your friends, families, and teachers that they were wrong about you, think of all the effort you will have gone through to win their approval; knowing that they care about you because of what you've accomplished, not who you are.

Then what is the right reason to pursue an acting career? Ask any successful actor. They'll all tell you the same thing. What keeps them going is an insatiable love of the work itself. They know that whether you're doing community theater or a Spielberg film, if you're doing what you love, you're living your dream, and what could be better than that? There's nothing wrong with fame and fortune, but if that's your primary motivation, you'd be better off robbing a bank.

*Being famous may give you a thrill for a little while but being gawked at by millions of strangers gets old pretty fast.*

## LIVING MOMENT TO MOMENT

One of the reasons there's a lot of depression and anxiety amongst the acting population is because actors often feel they can't live stimulating challenging lives until they've "made it." They forget that all an artist can bring to the work is what they draw from their lives and if their lives are spent waiting for the phone to ring, what they bring to the work will be severely limited.

Live your life in a way that stimulates, challenges, and excites you now, not just when your agent calls. Whether it's sky-diving, playing an instrument, writing, meditation, visiting museums, reading history, getting involved in a political cause, doing volunteer work or creating your own acting projects, live your life the way you would if you already had the career you wanted. You'll not only get where you want to go more quickly, but you'll enjoy the journey more.

*If your life is spent fretting and biting your fingernails waiting for "it" to happen, what you manifest in your art will be limited. If your life is vibrant and full of passion that will show up in your work.*

# FOR INFORMATION ON PRIVATE AND GROUP ON-CAMERA WORKSHOPS

# &

# ONE DAY AND WEEKEND INTENSIVES IN THE U.S. AND CANADA

Contact:
Doug Warhit at (310) 479-5647.
Or visit his website:www.dougwarhit.com